HOLIDAY MAGIC

*The Art of Making Decorations
for Eventful Days Throughout the Year*

HOLIDAY MAGIC

❀ ❀ ❀ ❀ ❀

*The Art of Making Decorations
for Eventful Days
Throughout the Year*

MARGARET PERRY

Photographs and Drawings by the Author

DOUBLEDAY & CO., INC., GARDEN CITY, NEW YORK

ISBN 0-385-12322-1

LIBRARY OF CONGRESS CATALOG CARD NUMBER 77–80908

Printed in the United States of America

CONTENTS

INTRODUCTION

EVER SINCE the beginning of time, man has celebrated certain events of the year—events such as the arrival of the winter solstice, when the days begin to lengthen after the dark days of early winter, and the start of the spring season, when all life is renewed.

For long centuries the celebrations through the year were religious occasions, and thus were known as "holy days." In more recent times, the year has been marked by festivals of both religious and secular importance, and although the original term for these events has been kept, it has evolved into the word "holidays," particularly for non-religious celebrations.

Holidays punctuate the year for us, bringing a welcome change in the steady pace of our day-to-day living routine. We plan for these holidays carefully, anticipate them with pleasure, enjoy them, and then put them aside for another year. And as these holidays arrive, year after year, they bring with them traditions that we have created to give each celebration a particular meaning—traditions in food, in decorations, in greetings for friends and family. Although most of us follow the general customs, we add to them and change them as years go by, and thus bring to each festival day a significance that has meaning for ourselves.

Making our own decorations is one of the best ways of bringing life to these events, giving our own expression to the centuries-old ceremonies and the traditions that have grown up around them. With many simple kinds of materials—paper, glue, scissors, ribbons, and a little imagination—we can create our own traditions as we celebrate the holidays around the year that begins with New Year's Eve.

HOLIDAY MAGIC

*The Art of Making Decorations
for Eventful Days Throughout the Year*

New Year's Eve

December 31/January 1

THE CELEBRATING of the New Year has always been a time for rejoicing, whether it was in the days when spring signaled the renewing of life on earth and thus the start of a new year, or the time of the harvest, when one crop was brought in and hopes were high for the crops of the year to come. All the old demons were chased away by the noisy merrymaking, assuring the incoming twelve months of a good beginning for a year of great fortune for everyone.

Today, friends and families gather at New Year's time to celebrate this renewing of the spirit and reviving of good cheer. A family dinner is traditional on New Year's Day, but it is on the night before, New Year's Eve, that the merrymaking reaches its peak as the hour of midnight approaches and everyone offers best wishes for the year ahead.

Through the years holiday decorations have played their part in the telling of why we rejoice at the ending of one year and the beginning of the next. We prepare a buffet table to be enjoyed as midnight approaches, with champagne almost always a part of the refreshments. The drinking of a toast to the New Year has become one of the most important parts of the ritual; fireworks at midnight play a part in the night-long celebration in many cities. Father Time, who, although only a year old, has grown a long white beard, is sent on his way, and the New Year, symbolized by a cupid in swaddling clothes, is welcomed as the harbinger of a good year to come.

FANCY HATS
FOR NEW YEAR'S EVE

ONE OF the traditional features of a New Year's Eve party is the wearing of fancy hats. They are freely distributed at restaurants and clubs, and if you are celebrating at home there should be fancy hats too. Here are a few designs that are easy to make and easy to wear. All you need is construction paper of various colors, stick glue, and hat elastics to hold the creations in place.

For a peaked hat of dunce-cap style, start with a third of a circle of bright colored paper that will make a cone 12″ tall. Use the long end of a 12″ by 18″ piece of paper (see diagram). Form into a cone, and secure with stick glue.

Trim the edge of the hat with a double strip of crepe paper of a contrasting color, stretching the paper as you glue it onto the hat to form a sort of ruffle. At

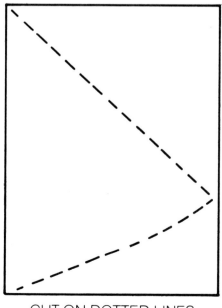

CUT ON DOTTED LINES

the peak, glue on a pompon made of a 12″ by 2″ strip of the contrasting paper rolled up and glued around the tip of the cone. Attach a hat elastic to keep the hat on.

A smaller version of this can be made with half of a 12″ circle. This will give you a wider cone and a hat that is easier to keep on, although it, too, needs an elastic.

To make a woman's crown, paste a ribbon onto a piece of gold paper cut in the shape of a tiara. Then tie the ribbon onto the lady's hairdo. The tiara can be decorated with cutouts or with rhinestones and sequins.

Napoleon's hat comes in colors of blue and red. Cut two pieces of blue construction paper of the same size—roughly 12″ long by 5″ wide, and shape it as shown in the photograph. Glue the two ends together, and trim with ½″ strips of red construction paper.

For a "sunbonnet Sue" hat, cut a large half circle, trim the curved edge with a ruffle of crepe paper, and glue two streamers to the corners for ties.

Make the hats in all colors, stand

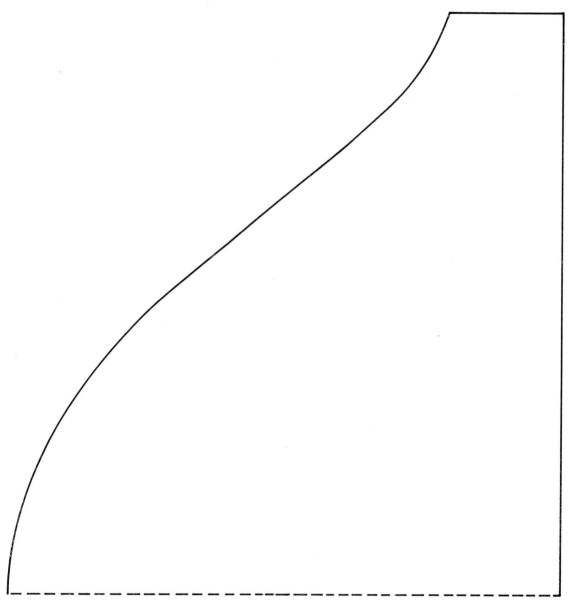

PLACE ON FOLD

them along the buffet table, and let each guest take the one of his choice.

NEW YEAR'S EVE CITY SCENE

As a background for your New Year's Eve party table, an icy cityscape sets the proper mood. Save all the boxes from your Christmas gifts and cover them with ice-blue wrapping paper. Snip little pieces of silver paper or a silver-paper doily and paste them on for windows and doors.

Trim the tops of your buildings with self-adhesive gold and silver braid, and

give some of them towers of silver. I used a silver top from a cologne bottle and the halves of a plastic silver egg of the sort that contains hosiery. And for the little round tower, I covered the container of a roll of 35mm film.

Arrange the buildings to stand at the back of your table, and let Father Time hold center stage.

OLD FATHER TIME

WHAT would a New Year's Eve buffet table be without Old Father Time pre-siding? He carries off the old year, cutting it clean with his scythe as the hour of midnight approaches.

Start with a half circle of white Bristol board or other plain white cardboard 6″ in diameter. Form the half circle into a cone and staple together. Snip off the top ½″ to make a place for the head to fit in.

Make arms of a strip of Bristol board about 6½″ long and ½″ wide. Secure at the back of the cone with masking tape, and bend them around toward the front. Father Time's long white hair will hide the masking tape.

For the head, choose a Brazil nut that has one smooth side for the face. Use white yarn for the shaggy eyebrows and a 2"-long beard. Attach with glue. Then glue on strands of white yarn for the hair, letting it fall in back to cover the shoulders where the arms are attached.

The scythe has a handle about 6" long, and a blade about 4" long, both cut from white Bristol board and decor-ated with strips of self-adhesive silver braid. Fasten the scythe in one hand with white glue.

Whatever your buffet centerpiece, be sure Old Father Time is in full view.

CHAMPAGNE TWOSOME

As the midnight hour approaches, the buffet table is set, the champagne

chilled and uncorked—all is ready for the welcoming of the New Year.

Let Mr. and Mrs. Champagne hold the stage as the buffet centerpiece. They are "bottle people," made with bottles wound with colored yarn and topped with "egg" heads—the plastic eggs used for hosiery containers.

Choose bottles 12" or 14" tall. Wind them with yarn of a shade to match your table decor, starting at the bottom. Secure the yarn with dabs of white glue as you go along.

Complete the heads before you glue them to the bottles. For the man's hair, glue on pieces of brown yarn, starting at the center top, filling one half of the egg and leaving the other half for the face. Trim the ends to make them even.

Out of black construction paper, cut a sweeping, curling mustache, and attach it with white glue. Experiment first with newspaper, until you have the shape you want. Give him sharp black eyebrows and oval black eyes, with a smaller white oval for the center. Attach with white glue.

For his hat, cut a strip of black construction paper 3½" by 9". Form a "stovepipe" for the crown by gluing the

short edges together. Glue this to the head, over the hair, and slip a ring of black construction paper over the crown to form the brim. The ring should be an oval 4″ by 5″ in size, with a hole approximately 2″ by 3″.

Give the lady a hairdo of yellow yarn. I've made bangs and pigtails tied with the same yarn. Oval black eyes and a half-moon-shaped mouth complete her face. Attach with white glue.

Next, attach the heads to the bottles. You can use white glue if your yarn winding has gone all the way to the very top of the bottle. If not, secure the heads with floral clay. I've found that this works very well.

A 1½″ by 6″ strip of white construction paper makes the man's collar. Glue it around the neck, with the seam at the back. Snip a ¼″ cut in the center front and turn down the tabs. Cut a black construction paper bow tie and glue to the collar.

The lady's collar is made of light blue construction paper, 1½″ by 6″, glued together at the back of the neck. Shape the front of the collar as shown in the photograph, and trim with blue lace, glued on.

NOISEMAKERS FOR NEW YEAR'S

GIVE each of your guests a handmade noisemaker for the magic hour of midnight, when with great enthusiasm the old year is ushered out and the new one invited in.

For these noisemakers save your typewriter ribbon boxes and other small metal containers.

First, place a few pebbles in the box, and fasten the cover securely with masking tape. Then wind an 18″-long piece of 12-gauge wire around the edge of the box, twist it together where it meets, and form a loop about 3″ long for a handle.

Sometimes I make the handle by twisting two pieces of wire together. And sometimes I paint the handles with gold paint.

Cover the box with bright felt or other colorful fabric, securing it with white glue. Trim with lace or a velvet ribbon around the edge of the box, and finish it off with a bow at the base of the handle.

Lincoln's Birthday

February 12

ABRAHAM LINCOLN was born on February 12, 1809, in a tiny log cabin in the backwoods of Kentucky. The little building, carried from its nearby original site, is now enshrined in an impressive monument just outside Hodgenville, protected for posterity from the vagaries of Kentucky's weather.

With virtually no formal schooling, Lincoln grew up to become the sixteenth President of the United States. He took office on March 4, 1861, winning, by a very slim margin, over his famous adversary, Stephen Douglas.

Lincoln's campaign platform recommended that slavery be excluded from the territories, a viewpoint strongly opposed by many states. Upon his election, several states withdrew from the Union, and on April 12, 1861, Confederate troops fired upon Fort Sumter at Charleston, South Carolina, setting off the Civil War.

Eventually, the Union was victorious, and Lincoln issued his famous Emancipation Proclamation.

Five days after the surrender of the Confederate Army and a month after his inauguration for a second term as President, Abraham Lincoln was assassinated. The bullet was fired by John Wilkes Booth during a performance at Ford's Theater in Washington, D.C., on Good Friday, April 14, 1865. The President died the next morning—on April 15.

One hundred years after Lincoln's birth the United States Congress directed that his birthday—February 12—be observed as a national holiday.

In recent years, celebrations on February 12 have included family luncheon and dinner parties, with appropriate table decorations. The little log cabin and the tall black hat that Lincoln always wore have become symbols that school children recognize as belonging to the President whose statue sits in the Lincoln Memorial in Washington, D.C.

THE LOG CABIN

THE log cabins in which Abraham Lincoln spent his childhood—and there were several of them as his family moved from place to place—always had a door and one small window in the front, with the chimney at the end near the window of the one-room building.

To make a model of such a cabin, start with a box about 6½″ wide, 8½″ long, and 3½″ high. If you can't find a box of the proper dimensions, cut a shoe box down to the size you want, which is what I did.

Cover the back of the cabin with a piece of corrugated cardboard that is 3½″ high by 8½″ long. Fasten it with Titebond Glue, or one of the white glues. Cut another piece of the same size for the front. In the center of the front cut out a piece for the door—about 1″ by 2¼″ Tape the door to the opening so it will swing *inward*, as such doors always seemed to do.

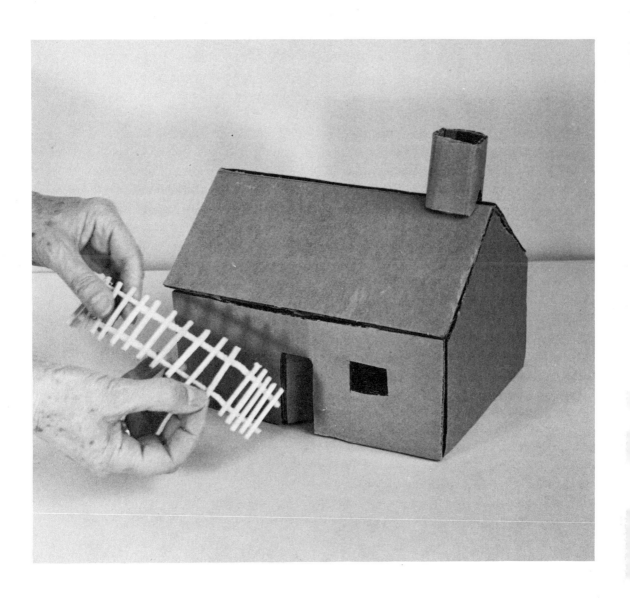

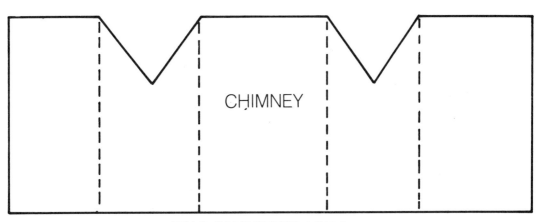

CHIMNEY

FOLD ON DOTTED LINES

Cut out a 1″-square opening for the window, aligning the top of the window with the top of the door. The window is about 1″ to the right of the door.

The side walls of the cabin form the peak on which the roof rests. Cut two pieces, each about 6½″ wide and 3½″ high at the sides (to match the front and back walls) and about 6½″ high at the peak. Glue these to the sides of the box.

The roof is an 8½″ by 8¾″ piece of cardboard. When you cut your roof, be sure the faint lines of the corrugated material run across the 8½″ length, so the effect will be that of a shingled roof. Also, it makes it easier to bend, as you will want to do, through the middle of the longer dimension.

Fit the roof onto the peaks of the sides, and attach with glue.

For the chimney, cut a piece of cardboard according to the pattern given, fold it on the dotted lines, glue it together, and glue it to the roof above and a little to the right of the window.

Lincoln always made split-rail fences, but picket fences were used in those days too. Start with white pipe cleaners for top and bottom rails. If the pipe cleaners aren't long enough to suit your scene, glue them together, overlapping the ends slightly. Cut the tops off burned-out kitchen matches for the pickets, and glue them to the pipe cleaners at about ¼″ intervals. For the gate, glue the pickets close together.

Place the cabin on a large piece of orange or brown construction paper, and landscape your scene with pine cones. If you have a small corn-husk doll, stand her in the front yard. And if you have a miniature owl, perch him in the pine cone "tree" as a symbol of Lincoln's great wisdom.

ABRAHAM LINCOLN
PARTY FAVORS

Marshmallow party favors for a Lincoln's birthday party can be put together easily and quickly.

Fasten together 3 large marshmallows, one on top of the other, with a toothpick. Paste a stovepipe hat on top, and paste on a little bow tie. Give the figure arms made of three tiny marshmallows fastened together with a toothpick.

For the top hat, cut an oval of black construction paper about 2″ long and 1½″ wide. On this glue a stovepipe made of black construction paper—a strip 1¾″ wide and 4″ long. Glue the shorter edges together.

Stand the figures around the party table, or make one for each guest and stand them at the place settings.

Valentine's Day

February 14

THIS IS the day, according to Geoffrey Chaucer, when birds choose their mates. Chaucer had a dream in which he came upon a hillside where all the birds had gathered. He says, in his *Parliament of Fowls*:

> For this was on Saint Valentine's day,
> When every bird cometh there to choose his mate.

We do not know for sure just who St. Valentine was, but legend has it that he was a Christian martyr in the third century. Just how his day has come to be the one on which lovers reaffirm their affection is lost in the mists of time. True it is, however, that friends and lovers send their greetings to one another on February 14, sometimes signing their cards and sometimes letting the lucky recipient guess who the sender is.

School children create their own valentines for their classmates as well as the trimmings for their classrooms. Gifts are often exchanged on Valentine's Day and parties given, and according to the folklore of the holiday, hearts, cupids, candy, and flowers are part of the decorations.

VALENTINE MOBILE

STRINGS of hearts suspended from a wire ring covered with red bias binding catch every whisper of breeze. Hang it in a doorway, above a party table, in a hallway or stairway.

Start with a piece of 12-gauge wire about 26″ long. Form it into a circle and secure with a piece of masking tape. This gives you a ring about 8″ across.

Cover the ring with red ribbon or red bias binding, fastening it with stick glue. Attach 3 pieces of black thread to the ring at equidistant points to suspend the mobile. Make the threads about 8″ long, and tie them together so they will hang from the knot and will be level.

The hearts on the strings are double, with black thread running in between. I used 5 hearts on 3 of the strings, using ever smaller hearts—and the kind that are self-adhesive. The strings are about 10″ long, and are hung halfway between each suspending thread. At the points where these 3 threads are attached, I hung a large heart on a 6″ piece of thread.

To complete the design, I attached a string of 5 small hearts from the knot by which the mobile is suspended.

VALENTINE PLACE SETTING

FOR a Valentine's Day luncheon party, here is a festive way to trim your table, and the whole setting takes only a few minutes to create.

Cut a large heart-shaped placemat out of white felt, about 14″ across at the widest part of the heart and about 11″ from top to bottom. Experiment first by cutting a pattern out of newspaper, until you have the shape you want.

Around the edge of the heart glue on a narrow red binding, and sprinkle red

hearts in a cluster at the left-hand top of the mat. Use the shiny, self-adhesive hearts that come in sheets. And, incidentally, keep the sheet after the hearts have been removed—the spaces make excellent stencils.

Make a coaster for the wine glass by covering a one-pound coffee can top or a jar top with red felt, and finish the edge with red bias binding to match the place-mat edging.

The place card is a 4″ square of plain white paper, folded in half so it will stand up, and decorated with hearts—a large red one, then a smaller gold one, and finally a small red one. For the napkin ring, make a circle of gold or red paper and trim it with a heart to match the place card.

VALENTINE PARTY FAVORS

AN ELEGANT, hand-held lady's mask for a Valentine's Day party is made of two layers of red construction paper.

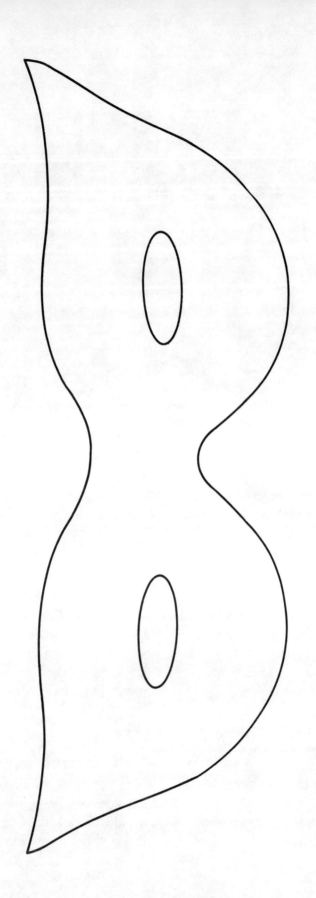

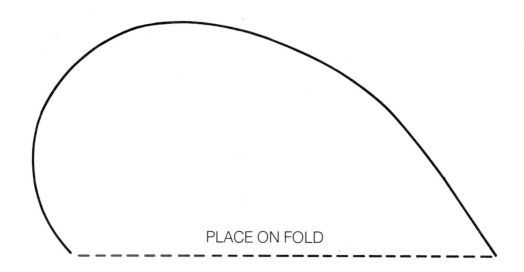

PLACE ON FOLD

Cut the mask according to the pattern given. Cut a piece of thin cardboard about 10″ long and 2″ wide for the handle. Glue this at the right-hand side of the mask between the two pieces, and paint it gold with acryllic paint or a felt pen.

Trim the eye openings and the corners of the mask with snips of lace paper doilies.

To go along with the mask, make a valentine fan. Use red construction paper for the heart-shaped favor. Experiment with newspaper until you have the shape and size you want (mine is about 5½″ by 6″), and use that for a pattern. Glue a handle of cardboard—about 1″ by 5″—between the two layers of the fan, and color the handle with paint or a felt pen. Trim with pieces of lace paper doily.

TABLE VALENTINE MOBILE

For a table decoration I made a small version of the hanging Valentine Mo-

bile, using fewer hearts on the strings and fewer strings.

I started with a piece of 12-gauge wire about 13″ long, and formed it into a circle, securing it with masking tape. This makes a ring about 4″ across. I covered the ring with red bias binding, gluing the binding to the wire with stick glue. Next, I attached 3 black threads, as with the large mobile, this time using threads about 6″ long, and knotting them together so the ring hangs evenly.

I put only 3 strings of hearts on the ring, spacing them evenly around the circle, and then hung a single heart on a black thread from the knot that suspends the mobile. The hearts are double, with black thread running between them.

For the table stand, cut a heart shape out of corrugated cardboard, making the shape about 6″ long at the longest point and about 6″ at the widest. Cover the heart with red felt—or paint it red with fast-drying enamel. Then edge the

start with plain cards and matching envelopes, and then create your own designs of colored paper and other materials such as gold braid, lace, ribbon, and yarn. Bookmarks, perhaps to enclose with a gift, also make colorful valentines.

The plain cards and envelopes are available at most art-supply shops. They come in a variety of colors, and they do give a handmade valentine a finished look. Here are a few suggestions for your designs.

Red and gold are traditional, of course, but try using pastels and lace for an old-fashioned valentine, with tiny bows of satin ribbon. Odds and ends from the family scrapbox can often be put to good use in making your own valentines.

For a simple valentine, start with a heart-shaped piece of red metallic paper. To get a pattern for your heart, experiment with newspaper, cutting out hearts until you have the size and shape you want.

Glue white lace around the edges of the red heart, gathering the lace as you glue. Then paste the heart onto a plain card—and your valentine is finished. Write your message on the inside of the card.

Another design can be made with strips of flowered lace. First, make a newspaper pattern of a heart, and trace around it onto your plain card. Then cut the lace strips to fit inside the traced heart, with the longest one in the middle and ever shorter pieces to each side. Trim the ends to conform to the heart shape.

Paste the strips in place, and glue an edging around the heart, using white

heart with red bias binding (or rickrack braid), attaching it to the cardboard with stick glue.

Using a 12″ piece of 12-gauge wire, bend a ½″ at right angles and insert it into the cardboard at the center top of the heart. Secure with masking tape and cover the tape with a red ribbon bow. If the wire goes all the way through, bend it flat against the underside of the cardboard and secure with masking tape.

Then bend the wire to form an arc, centering the top end of the wire over the heart-shaped base. Make a loop and suspend the mobile from it.

VALENTINES

MAKING valentines for a few favored friends can be fun, especially if you

yarn or gold cord. Finish with a small bow at the top of the heart.

If you happen to have lace that is wide enough, cut out a lace heart and paste it onto a plain card. White lace on a red card is very effective, with nothing more than a tiny bow at the top of the heart.

For a heart "tree," cut out 5 small hearts of gold or red metallic paper.

With a brown sharp-pointed felt pen, draw just a few lines suggesting branches of a tree on a plain card, and paste on the hearts as though they were growing on the tree.

Bookmarks are simple to make. Cut out a piece of heavy red or white paper about 2″ by 5″, punch a hole ½″ in from the narrow edge, and slip a piece of yarn or gold cord through the hole.

34

Tie a knot in the end of the cord. Then paste hearts of graduated sizes on the bookmark, using metallic paper for the hearts.

For a heart-shaped bookmark, cut out 2 hearts of heavy paper and glue them together with an edging of lace between them. Punch a hole at the top of the heart for a cord (or glue on a loop of red or white yarn).

Sheets of red hearts are available at stationery stores at Valentine's Day time. These hearts are useful in making valentines and bookmarks. But don't throw away the sheet from which the hearts have been removed—it makes an excellent stencil. With a felt pen and such a stencil, you can decorate valentines, bookmarks, place cards, and all sorts of gift cards.

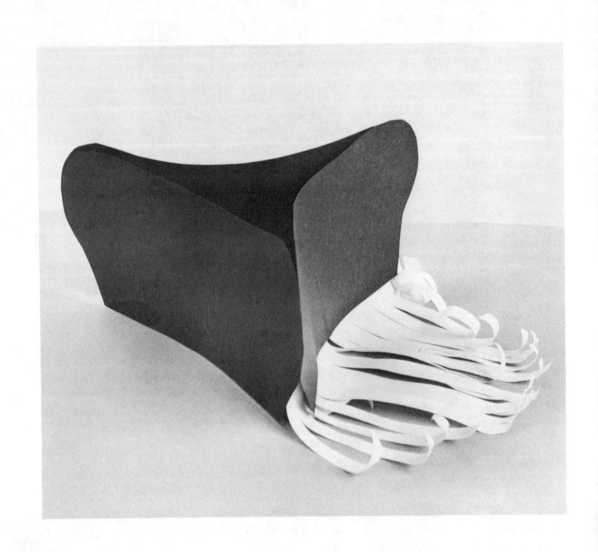

George Washington's Birthday

February 22

OUR first national hero, George Washington, was born on February 22, 1732, on a plantation known as Wakefield, in Westmoreland County, Virginia. Little is known of his early schooling except that it was sketchy, but Washington grew up to become an accomplished surveyor, an enthusiastic patriot, a great statesman, and a brilliant military commander. In 1789 he was unanimously elected as the first President of the newly created United States of America.

Ever since the days when Washington led us to independence, winning the Revolutionary War against the British, his birthday has been celebrated—a tradition carried to this country by the colonists from England, who had always celebrated the birth date of their king.

George Washington died in 1799, and one year later, in 1800, Congress passed a resolution marking February 22 as a day of commemoration for our first President.

Just how the legend of George Washington and the cherry tree started is not known, but the first mention of it, as far as we know, appeared in Parson Weems's Fable in 1806. The story goes that George, as a boy, chopped down a cherry tree and readily confessed that he had done it with his little hatchet, adding, "I cannot tell a lie."

The celebration of Washington's birthday, now officially set as the last Monday in February, has become one of the nation's more important holidays, with parties and family gatherings. It comes at a welcome time in the long winter months, and to make the occasion festive, decorations—including cherries and hatchets —are always part of the holiday buffet table, all telling the stories of the life of the Father of our Country.

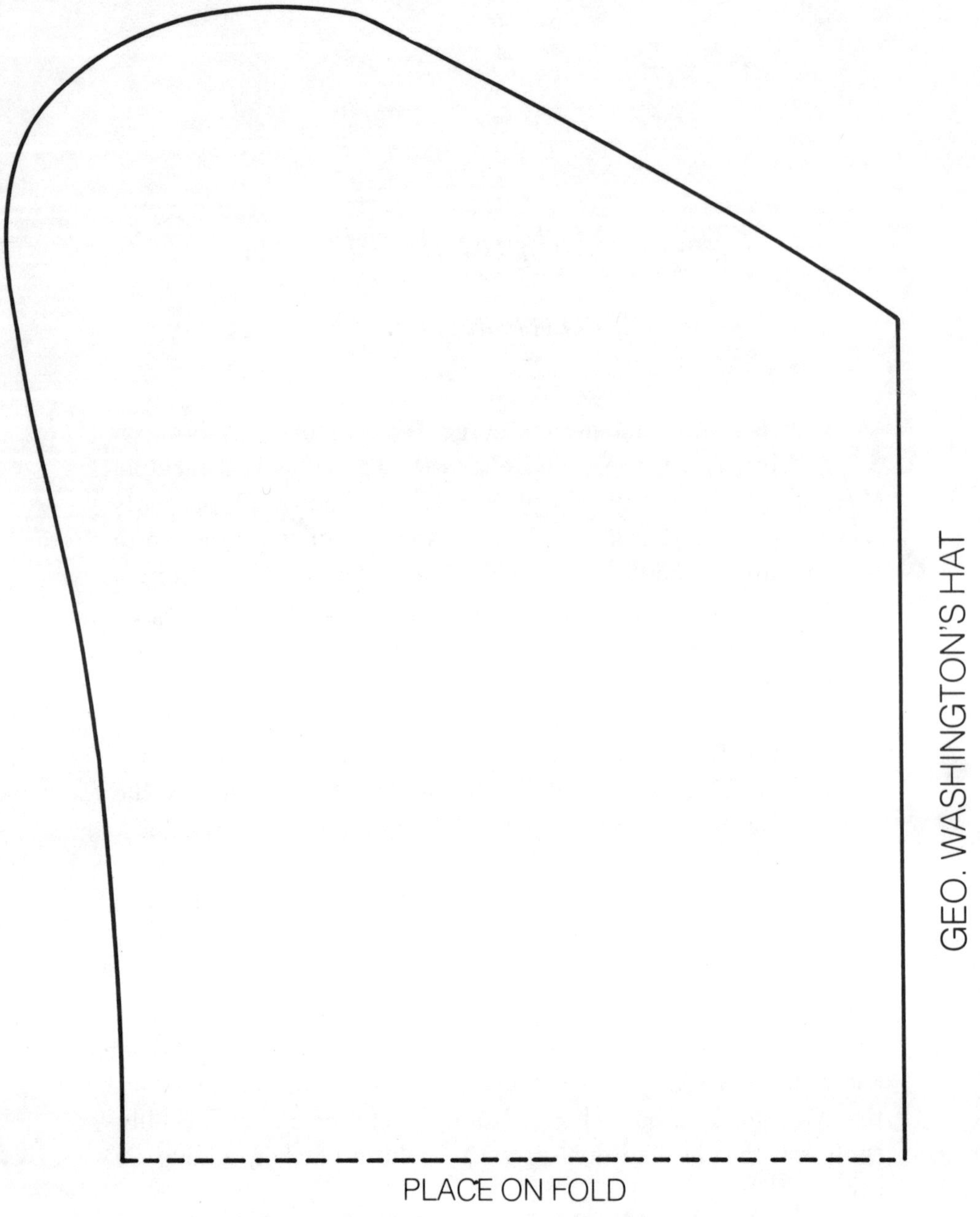

GEO. WASHINGTON'S HAT

PLACE ON FOLD

GEORGE WASHINGTON HATS

For the children at a George Washington party, tricorn hats in all colors—complete with paper perukes (wigs)—are always popular.

For the hat, cut 3 pieces of construction paper, following the pattern given. Glue the edges of the 3 pieces together to form a tricorn shape.

Make a peruke for the tricorn hat. Cut a piece of white or brown con-

38

struction paper long enough to extend
the length of the back third of the hat
and about 6″ deep, curving the piece
slightly on the bottom edge. Make slits
about every ½″, without cutting all the
way through, and curl up the "hair" on
a pencil. Glue the peruke to the back of
the hat.

WASHINGTON'S BIRTHDAY PLACE MATS

A BUNCH of cherries and red rickrack
braid trim a white felt place mat for a
Washington's Birthday party. Cut the
felt 18″ long and 12″ wide, and glue on
a trimming of red braid. Use stick glue—
it holds well and will not damage the
felt. Cut cherries out of red felt, leaves
and stems of green felt, and glue these
to the upper left-hand corner of the
mat. It's quick and colorful, and the felt
protects the table finish.

Purim

February–March

THIS IS a joyful celebration of the Jewish people, a holiday of revelry commemorating the saving of the Jews by Queen Esther.

The beautiful Esther, married to the Persian King, Ahasuerus, learns from her cousin Mordecai that the King's councilman, Haman, has persuaded the King to destroy all the Jews. Esther intercedes with the King, the Jews are saved, and the wicked Haman is hanged.

Ever since the days of Queen Esther, Purim has been a happy time for Jewish people around the world, a time commemorated by parties and festivities and joyous merrymaking, particularly by the children.

Hamantaschen, a triangular-shaped pastry symbolic of Haman's hat, has a filling of sweets—traditionally, poppyseeds, but in recent years, apricot and other fruits. Kreplach, too, are popular—triangular pastries with a meat filling. Beans and salt, said to have been Esther's diet at the Persian court to avoid violating the Jewish dietary laws, are sometimes served.

On Purim the children dress up in costumes and make merry the whole day long. One dresses as Queen Esther, with crown and robe; another as King Ahasuerus, also in a crown. Mordecai is represented, and the wicked Haman comes out in a long black coat and a black triangular hat. He is chased by the others, who try to hit him with "hit Haman" bean bags.

CROWNS FOR QUEEN ESTHER AND KING AHASUERUS

THESE are the two characters who take part in the festival of Purim, parading in their costumes and shaking their noise-makers every time Haman's name is mentioned.

Use a metallic paper for the crowns. I've made Queen Esther's pink and the King's silver. Measure the child's head, allow 2″–3″ more for overlapping, and

PLACE ON FOLD

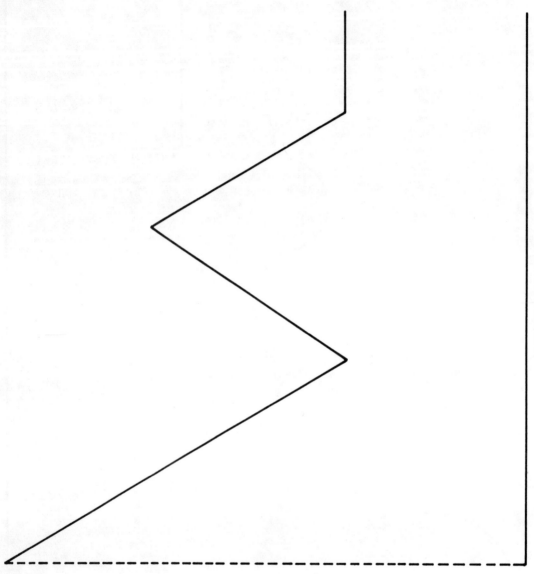

KING'S CROWN

PLACE ON FOLD

cut a strip to that same measure about 6″ wide.

Cut the designs (see patterns) into the front of the crowns, and make the rest of the headpiece about 2″ wide. Fasten with glue or tape at the back. Trim the crowns with self-adhesive gold or silver braid.

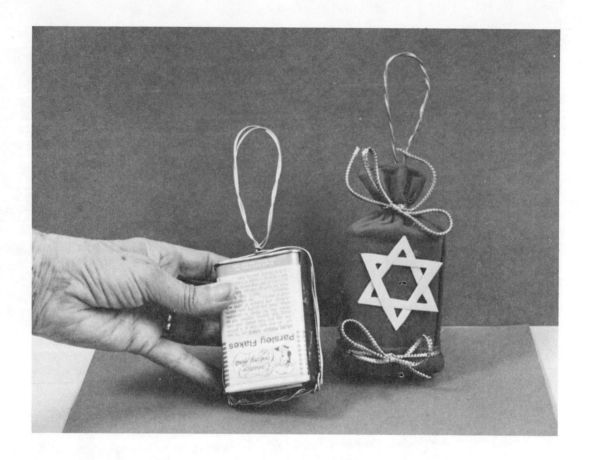

NOISEMAKERS FOR PURIM

DURING the festival of Purim the story is told of the horrid Haman, the traitor who tried to trick Queen Esther. Every time Haman's name is mentioned, the children rattle their noisemakers or gragers to drown out the sound.

Here is a noisemaker that is easy to put together. Start with an empty Band-Aid tin, or some other small tin box. Put a few pebbles in it and tape the cover on tightly. Then wind a double piece of 12-gauge wire around the box and make a loop for a handle—without cutting the wire. Twist firmly at the base of the handle.

Cover the box with bright-colored felt, attaching it with white glue. Tie a bow of gold braid, or a ribbon to match the felt, around the handle, and trim with a golden Star of David.

To make the Star of David, cut out two gold-paper triangles, all sides equal, and snip out the center of each so only ¼″ remains all around the triangle. Fit the triangles together by slipping a point of one under the side of the other. Paste to the felt-covered box.

THE MEGILLAH

THIS is a scroll, a single scroll, on which the story of Esther is written. To put together a Megillah you will need a pair of wooden spools and a ¼″ dowel about 9″ long. An unsharpened pencil will also do, but the dowel makes a better-looking Megillah.

Glue a spool onto each end of the dowel, letting about a ½″ extend beyond the spool. Color the spools with brown acryllic paint or with a brown felt pen.

Cut a strip of white shelf paper about 2 yards long and 5½″ wide—wide enough to just fit onto the dowel. Glue one end of the strip to the dowel and wind it up. At the other end paste on a piece of colored paper—preferably one with an interesting design on it—for the cover of the scroll. Attach a ribbon to the cover to tie the scroll securely.

Then let each child write his own story of Esther. If it is to be told in Hebrew, the scroll should be rolled up from right to left. If in English, roll it from left to right.

The children can illustrate their story of Esther with drawings of the Queen and the other people in the story, or with cutouts pasted onto the scroll.

47

The Champagne Twosome, bottle people, welcome the
guests to the New Year's Eve party.

Fancy hats for New Year's Eve, made of construction
paper, are trimmed with a contrasting color.

Valentine mobile, made of
strings of hearts, hangs in
a doorway or stairwell to
catch the air currents.

An assortment of valentines can be made with laces,
ribbons and hearts pasted to plain cards.

Purim party favors include crowns for Queen Esther
and King Ahasuerus, noisemakers, and megillahs.

Valentine bookmarks,
some long and narrow, some
heart-shaped, have loops
of yarn or gold cord.

Carnations, leprechauns and shamrocks along with tiny
top hats trim a St. Patrick's Day party table.

An Easter egg tree, made of branches secured in plaster
of Paris, holds an entire collection of fancy eggs.

St. Patrick's Day

March 17

S T. PATRICK, patron saint of Ireland, has given us one of the
year's jolliest holidays. It is, of course, a religious celebration,
as St. Patrick brought Christianity to the Emerald Isle. But he is
said to have performed so many miracles and delivered the Irish
people from so many miseries that it has become for all of us a
happy occasion.

Just why March 17 was chosen as his day is not known, as we
do not know the date of either St. Patrick's birth or death. But
certain it is that he presided over the Christian church in Ireland
during the fifth century.

A legend tells us that St. Patrick used a shamrock—because of
its three equal leaves—to explain the Christian Trinity, the Father, the Son, and the Holy Spirit. And to this day the shamrock
is a symbol of the deeds of St. Patrick.

Because March 17 is an Irish holiday, and a happy one, leprechauns, as well as shamrocks, usually appear in the table trimmings of St. Patrick's Day parties. These Irish elves, according to
legend, are tiny old shoemakers. If you catch one, he will lead
you to a hidden treasure. The white clay pipes these elves smoke
as they hammer away on their shoes also find their way into St.
Patrick's Day decorations.

GREEN CARNATION BOUQUET

FOR a St. Patrick's Day party centerpiece, arrange a bouquet of green paper
carnations in a basket or a large vase.

To make the flower, cut a strip of
green tissue paper (or crepe paper)
about 12″ long and 5″ wide. Double it
lengthwise, and snip it at ¼″ intervals
along the doubled edge. Run a ribbon
of white glue (use very little) along the
uncut edge, and wind the flower around

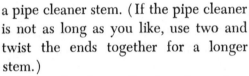

a pipe cleaner stem. (If the pipe cleaner is not as long as you like, use two and twist the ends together for a longer stem.)

When the glue is dry (it takes only a few minutes), wrap floral tape around the base of the flower and wind it down the stem, completely covering the pipe cleaner. It will stick to itself.

After your bouquet is finished, make extra carnations for your guests, but use short stems for these.

ST. PATRICK'S DAY
PARTY FAVORS

LITTLE green leprechauns' hats filled with nuts or candy trim a St. Patrick's Day party table.

Kelly-green Bristol board works well for these little hats. Cut an oval about 3″ wide and 4″ long for the base of the hat—actually, the brim. Form a top-hat crown of a strip of Bristol board 6″ long and 2½″ wide. Glue it together, short edge to short edge, and then glue it to the oval base. Leave the top open for the nuts or candy.

To trim the hat, cut a strip of black construction paper ½″ wide and 7″ long, and glue it around the hat near the base. Onto this, in the front, glue a black shamrock (see pattern), and your party favor is complete. Make one for each guest.

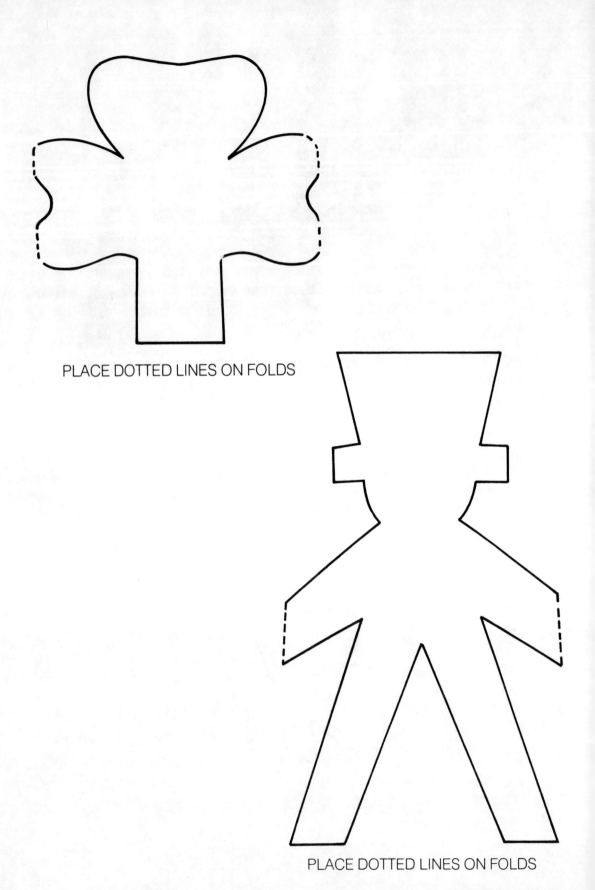

PLACE DOTTED LINES ON FOLDS

PLACE DOTTED LINES ON FOLDS

ST. PATRICK'S DAY PARTY TABLE TRIMS

To SET off your centerpiece, cut out a leprechaun or a shamrock table trim. Start with a strip of green construction paper and fold it into 3″ sections.

Cut the folded paper according to the patterns given, making sure that at one place you do not cut through the sides, so the figures will hold together. Open it up—and you have your table trim.

If your construction paper is not long enough to give you the trim you want, make two or more, and tape them together with invisible Scotch Tape.

53

Easter

March 22–April 25

EASTER Sunday is the most important holy day in the Christian year. This is the day on which Jesus is believed to have risen from the dead, three days after His crucifixion. The date of Easter changes from year to year, according to a system established in the year 325 by the Council of Nicaea, which had been convened by the Roman Emperor Constantine. The Council decreed that Easter would fall on the first Sunday after the first full moon after the vernal equinox (the first day of spring). Thus, Easter can fall on any Sunday from March 22 to April 25.

Not only has Easter religious significance for us, it is a time to rejoice that the long winter months have passed and the return of spring is at hand, a time when all life is renewed and faith and hope reaffirmed. Family and friends gather for special dinner parties, children's egg hunts, and parades of Easter finery. The custom of wearing new clothes signifies a new beginning.

Most popular of the Easter symbols are the rabbit and the egg —both representing fertility and the renewing of life. Actually, it was the hare, not the rabbit, that traditionally symbolized Easter, as the hare since pagan times has been considered a symbol of the moon—it is nocturnal like the moon, it is said not to ever close its eyes at night, and it carries its young for a month before giving birth. And because the date of Easter depends on the moon, the hare was chosen as a secular representation of the holy day.

The two creatures, the hare and the rabbit, are, of course, close relatives, and in America the rabbit came to be the Easter creature that brings gifts to the children and colored eggs for their Easter baskets.

Table decorations for the traditional Easter dinner include these symbols, as do Easter greeting cards.

EASTER BASKETS

THERE are several ways to make your own Easter baskets. And the ones you make yourself are usually much more attractive than those ready-made ones found in the shops.

The little plastic strawberry and vegetable baskets found in the markets serve well as a base. To decorate the basket, cut 3″ circles of pastel-colored tissue paper. Cut several layers at a time, and scallop the edges. Then fold the circles into quarters without creasing them, and tuck into the openings in the plastic basket. Use three or four circles together. These will stay secure without glue.

Fasten on two pipe cleaners twisted together to make a sturdy handle. Use a color that blends with the tissue paper. Fill the basket with shredded tissue

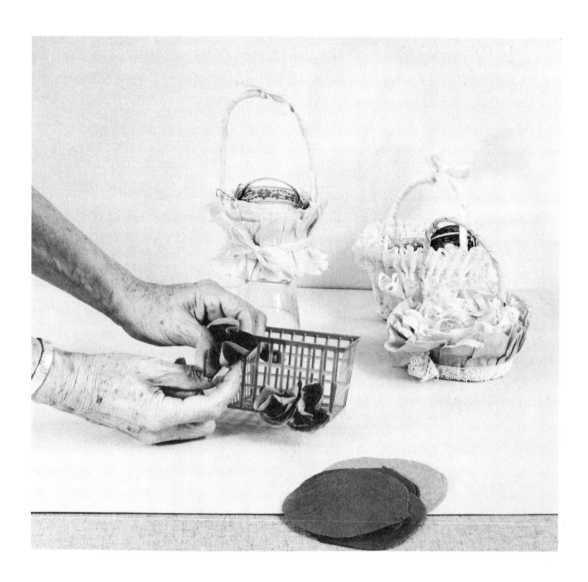

paper for the "grass," and put colored Easter eggs into the basket.

Also excellent for Easter baskets are the plastic margarine containers. Poke a hole with scissors on each side near the top through which to fasten the handle. Trim with pastel crepe-paper ruffles glued to the sides, and fasten on a pipe cleaner handle of harmonizing color. Finish the basket with ribbon or lace.

For an elegant Victorian design, cover the plastic container with rows of pink-edged white eyelet embroidery. First run a pink ribbon through the eyelets, and gather the fabric to make a ruffle. Then glue it to the sides of the container. I used two rows of embroidery for mine.

Attach a handle made of pipe cleaner and wound with white yarn, and tie a pink velvet bow to the top. Fill with "grass" and colored Easter eggs. This one will become a family heirloom.

EASTER EGG TREE

ONCE you start to decorate Easter eggs, it is hard to stop. There are an infinite variety of colors, designs, and materials to work with, from paints to felt pens and from laces to beads. If you keep your eggs and add to them each year, you will soon have a valuable collection.

To blow out the inside of a raw egg, pierce each end with a needle or sharp point of small manicure scissors. Prick the yolk with a needle so it will run out easily.

Make one hole a very little bit larger than the other, and blow through the smaller one, forcing the contents of the egg out through the larger one. Rinse out the egg shell with water and let it dry thoroughly.

To color the egg, paint it with water-soluble acrylic paint—these come in several bright colors. Or you can use regular water colors. Bright-colored felt pens also work well.

Then trim the egg with ribbon, lace, cutouts, decals, beads, or whatever your design calls for. I covered some of mine with calico, fastening it with white glue, and then I covered the seams with white rickrack braid. Another one I painted coral color, circled with light blue ribbon, which I pasted on, and then attached tiny seed pearls (from the five-and-ten-cent store) to the rib-

bon. And another I painted gold and put nothing on it except a small spray of gold leaves at the top.

For the tree on which to hang your decorated eggs, collect some branches from your garden or from the woods—branches without leaves—and arrange them in a coffee can filled with plaster of Paris. In a few minutes the branches will be fast and completely secure in the plaster.

To prepare the plaster, mix the dry white powder with water to a soft doughlike consistency. The plaster grows warm as it dries, and the ten minutes or so that it takes to harden will give you time enough to arrange your branches.

Cover the can with construction paper, and if you want to decorate it, you might cut out a collection of egg-shaped pieces of pastel colors and glue them onto the can.

Hang your decorated eggs on your tree—and your centerpiece or hallway table will be ready to greet your holiday visitors.

If you prefer to stand your colorful Easter eggs on a table or mantel, cut strips of gold or silver stiff paper about 3″ long and ¾″ wide, form into a ring, fasten with glue, and place your egg into the ring. Bottle caps, too, make stands for eggs and can be painted with either gold or silver paint. They should be about 1″ across to hold the egg.

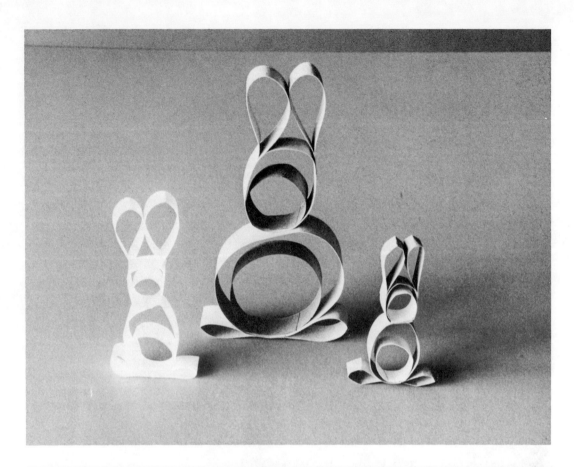

EASTER BUNNIES

A BEVY of Easter bunnies makes easy decorations for a buffet table. They can also be used as place cards. These colorful animals are made of strips of colored paper—construction paper and, for the larger ones, Bristol board. Whatever paper you use, make sure it is colored on both sides, as the insides of the strips will show.

For the small bunny standing about 4″ high, cut strips ¼″ wide. The body takes a strip 5½″ long, formed into a circle, and secured with stick glue. Inside this ring make another one, this time using a strip 3½″ long. Make each one of a different color. I used pale green and yellow.

For the head, use a 3″ strip glued to form a ring, with a 2″ circle inside. The ears are made of 3″ strips (green), looped in half (not creased), and glued to the head. The feet are a green 5½″ strip, looped to each side, and glued to the body. This makes the bunny stand up by himself.

I made my rabbits in three sizes. The ones that stand 6″ tall take ½″-wide strips: 8″ long for the body, with a 5½″ strip for the circle inside; 4½″ for the head, with a 3½″ circle inside; 4″ for the ears; 6″ for the feet.

The larger ones, made of Bristol board, stand 8½″ high. They are made of inch-wide strips: 13″ long for the body, with a 10½″ circle inside; 8½″ long for the head, with a 6″ circle in-

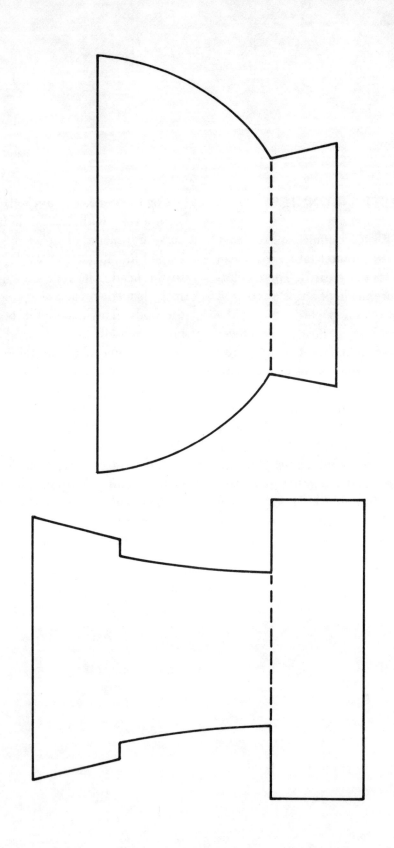

side; 6″ for the ears; and 9″ for the feet.

I used two colors for each bunny and used stick glue to put the various parts together.

If you want to make place cards, glue the body to one end of a flat strip about 6″ long, and attach an egg-shaped piece of paper to the other end of the base for the name.

EASTER PLACE CARDS

For the Easter dinner party, make a collection of flower pots full of spring flowers as place cards. They are as decorative as miniature flower arrangements and useful as well.

Use colored construction paper for the pots. Cut 2 of each, following the pattern given. Then snip green leaves and stems, and cut flower shapes of various colors. Attach the blossoms to the stems with stick glue, arrange the flowers and leaves in between the two pots, and secure with stick glue. At the side of the pot, slip a small card in between the two cutouts, and glue it in place. Write the name of the guest on this card.

To make the place card stand up,

bend each pot at right angles along the dotted lines so that one flap extends to the back of the card and one to the front of the card.

EASTER GREETING CARDS

ONE OF the most popular times of the year to send greeting cards to friends and family is Easter time. And if the cards are handmade, they are especially appreciated.

Here are a few design suggestions. For the card itself, buy those with matching envelopes. They are available in several colors at art-supply shops.

Designs can be cut from bright-colored construction paper and secured to the cards with stick glue. For the pot of spring flowers shown here, follow the pattern of the pot given for the Easter place cards, and cut off the base at the dotted line. Cut green leaves and stems, and snips of colored paper for blossoms. These should be put on the card first, attaching them with stick glue, and then the pot is placed on the stems, so the flowers look as though they are growing in the pot.

The large Easter egg is made of strips of pink-flowered lace mounted on a card of pastel green. I cut an egg shape of pink construction paper, 4½″ high and 3″ wide at the widest point, pasted this on the card, and then put on the 3 strips

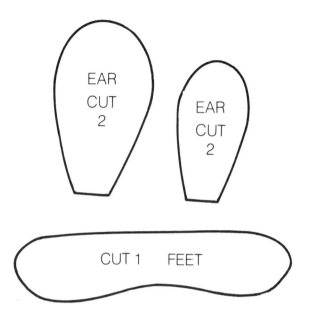

EAR
CUT
2

EAR
CUT
2

CUT 1   FEET

of lace. Around the edge of the egg I glued on gold braid and put a strip of the braid between the lace pieces. To finish off the card, I made a bow of the gold braid and glued it securely to the top of the egg.

The Easter bunny cards are made of 2 pastel colors on a card of contrasting color. Follow the patterns given for the ears and feet. The head is a circle 1½" in diameter, with a smaller circle—1" in diameter—of a second color. The body of the bunny is a circle 2¼" in diameter, with a second circle—1¼" in diameter—of the second color. I used pink and green on a blue card, and pink and green on a yellow card.

Assemble the bunny as shown in the photograph. The ears are placed with the smaller one on top. The feet are glued under the body so only the ends of the feet show.

Passover

March–April

PASSOVER, or Pesach, commemorates for the Jewish people their exodus from the land of Egypt, where they had been held in slavery. God had ordered each Jewish household to slaughter an unblemished lamb from its flock, and to sprinkle its blood on the doorpost. They were then to eat the roasted lamb in preparation for their journey out of Egypt. That night an angel of God came to slay all the first born of Egypt, "passing over" those homes that had the blood of the lamb on them, thus sparing the Jews from the decree.

This eight-day religious celebration starts with a Seder, a ritual family meal, which is repeated on the second night of Passover. During the Seder the story of the Exodus is told, each member of the family reading from the Haggada, the book that contains the account of the episode.

Ceremonial foods are prepared for the Seder, including a roasted lamb bone, a hard-boiled egg, bitter herbs, and greens, each one symbolic of the events of their journey out of Egypt. Matzah, unleavened bread, is served and eaten throughout the week of Passover. It represents the bread that, baked in haste before the Jews fled, did not have time to rise and was therefore flat, or unleavened.

Decorations for the Seder table follow the traditions of the story, as the ritual proceeds, and the family joins together to commemorate the occasion.

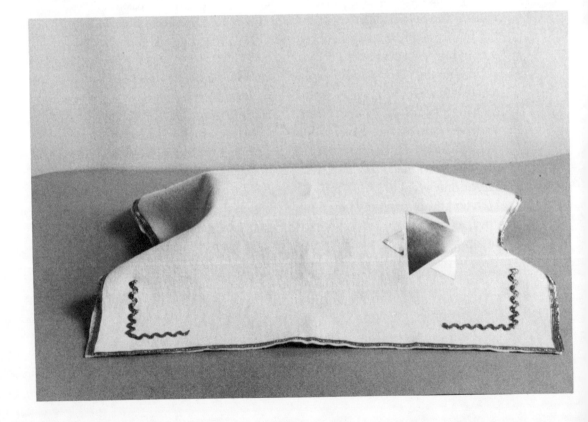

A BOX FOR THE HAGGADA

EACH member of the family should have his own Haggada when the evening of the celebration of Passover arrives, the evening of the first Seder. To keep these books together and ready for the occasion, here's a box designed especially for them. It will preserve them for the year to come.

Cover a wooden cigar box, or other box large enough to hold your Haggadas, and cover it with white felt or with dark blue paper. On the cover of the box paste cutouts of the word "Haggada" so everyone knows that inside are the texts that will be used for the family Seder.

MATZAH COVER

TRADITIONALLY, a special covering is made for the matzah at Passover time, to be used for the Seder.

This one is decorative and elegant in its simplicity. It is made of a 16″ square of white felt. The edges are trimmed with a fringed gold braid, put on with white glue.

Each corner of the cover is accented with gold rickrack, also glued on, and the Star of David, cut out of gold metallic paper, is glued in one corner. After the Seder, the cover can be folded and put away for future use.

May Day

May 1

WE don't know the origin of this happy holiday, but we do know that it goes back to prehistoric times, when the flowers began to bloom in the spring and the trees put forth their leaves—a joyful time of the year when all the world was fresh and beautiful.

For centuries it has been the custom of villages to put up a maypole on the first day of May, and for the townspeople to dance around it, carrying garlands of flowers they have gathered in the woods. In England a Queen of the May was chosen from the young girls of the village to preside over the ceremonies. In America some of the colleges carry on this tradition, crowning their Queen of the May to lead the festivities.

In the northern countries, the ceremony of the maypole takes place on the longest day of the year, when the weather has turned warm and the trees and flowers are in bloom. In Sweden, for instance, the maypole (*maistang*) is put up on *Midsummer Dagen* in every city, town, and village, and the people, young and old, gather to dance around it to the tunes of traditional folk music played by two or three accordionists, with dancers and musicians wearing traditional costumes.

The Swedish maypole, unlike the ones found in America today, has a crosspiece from which two large circles, symbols of eternity and fertility, are suspended, all decorated with leaves and flowers. As you drive through the countryside on this summer holiday you find the colorful festival in full swing at every tiny town.

In America, school children dance around the maypole, each child holding a colored streamer fastened to the top of the pole.

With half the group going one way and half the other, they weave a colored covering for the pole.

May baskets, too, are part of the present-day celebration. The children make their little baskets, gather wildflowers to fill them, and hang them on the doors of their friends.

THE MAYPOLE

As A party centerpiece, a miniature maypole is easy to make with simple materials.

For the base, cut a circle of light green Bristol board—or any cardboard—about 14″ across, and mark the center point. If you can't find green cardboard, cut the same-sized circle of light green crepe paper and cover the cardboard. Secure with spots of stick glue.

For the pole, glue pink crepe paper around a paper towel cardboard tube—you will probably need two layers, and use stick glue.

For the winding of the pole you will need 6 narrow ribbons—3 of one color and 3 of another. I used blue and pink satin ribbon about ½″ wide. Cut each piece about 15″ long. Alternating the colors, glue one end of the ribbons inside the top of the cardboard tube at equal intervals.

In the top of the tube glue a rosette made of long strips of the pink paper rolled up and ruffled slightly at the edges.

Six little figures stand around my maypole holding the ribbons. I've made my figures in two different ways. They all stand about 3½″ high, and all are in pastel shades.

Three figures have bodies made of half of a 5″ circle of paper, stapled to form a cone. I've used metallic paper to give the scene brilliance, but construction paper works well too. Snip off

about a ¼″ of the point of the cone, and then using white glue, attach an acorn or other small nut onto the top of the cone for the head.

Make a small hole on each side of the body about ¾″ down from the top, and slip a 4″ piece of pipe cleaner through for the arms. Turn up one end so it will hold the ribbon.

For the hats, make small cones, or poke bonnets, to match their costumes and glue them in place.

Three of my figures are "pine cone people"—their bodies are small pine cones with wide paper skirts attached. Their heads are acorns.

Choose a pine cone no more than 1½″ long. The skirt is half of a 5″ circle, with about 1″ of the center cut out. With the scales of the pine cone pointing downward, slip the skirt up into the scales until it fits all around. Then glue it together at the back and put a few drops of glue up into the scales to hold the skirt secure.

The arms are 4″ pieces of pipe cleaners slipped into the scales at the back.

Put the head on with white glue, and hold it carefully for a few minutes. Once the glue has set, it will hold the head securely. If you have an acorn that still has its cap, leave it on for the hat.

Put a ribbon in the hand of each little

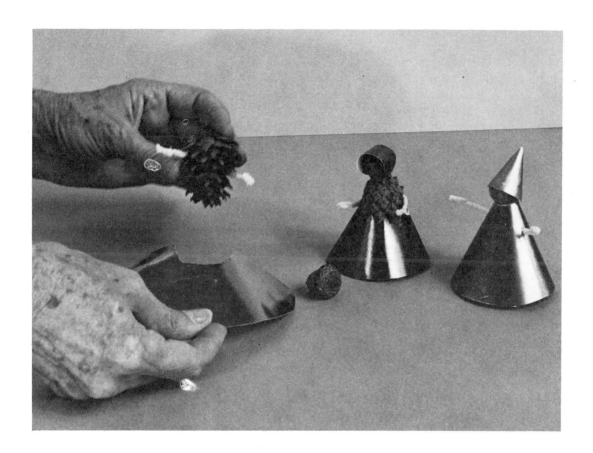

figure. Face every other one in the opposite direction, and let them weave a
little way down the pole, if you like.
I've left mine unwoven as the ribbon
seems to fall better that way.

MAY BASKETS

TRADITIONALLY, May baskets are simple
little paper baskets made by the children themselves to be given to their fa-
vorite friends. They are colorful and just
large enough to hold a few wildflowers
—or, if wildflowers are not easily found,
a few pansies, pinks, or other small garden blossoms. The baskets, pasted to-

gether and well-filled, are hung on the
doorknobs of friends, sometimes with
the giver's name on the baskets, and
sometimes without it.

One of the easiest ways to make a
May basket is to start with a 6″ square
of colored paper. Draw lines across all
four sides of the square 1½″ in from the
edges. This will give you a 3″ square in
the middle of the paper. Cut along dotted lines in the pattern given, and fold
on all lines. Paste the sides together to
form the basket.

Cut a strip of the same or contrasting
paper ½″ wide and 8″ long. Paste to the
opposite sides of the basket to form the
handle.

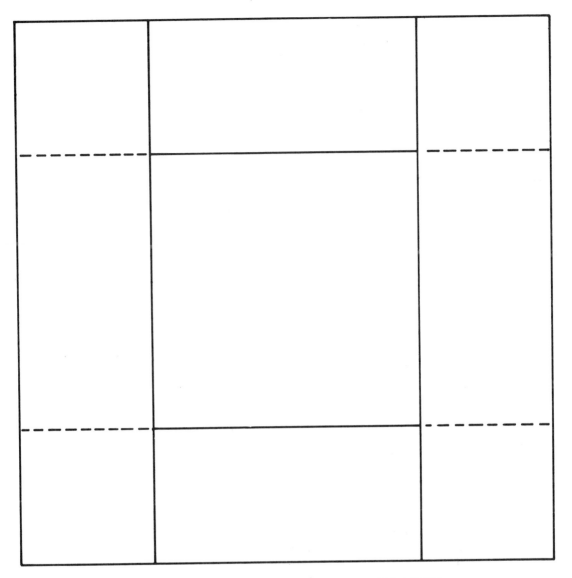

CUT ON DOTTED LINES—FOLD ON ALL LINES

To decorate the basket, draw an edging with a magic marker, or paste on pieces of paper lace doilies.

Another simple basket is made of a 6″ paper lace doily. Cut out a pie-shaped piece, leaving three quarters of the doily to form a wide cone. Paste it together, line it with a colored paper or with another doily, and fasten a pipe cleaner to opposite sides of the cone for a handle.

For a May Day party, hang flower-filled baskets on branches cut from a shrub or tree. Secure the branches in a vase, a coffee can, or a flower pot with sand, pebbles, or crushed newspaper. Let each child take home a basket as a souvenir of the party.

Mother's Day

Second Sunday in May

THE celebration of a day in May to honor mothers was started in 1908 by Anne M. Jarvis, who spent her life caring for her own mother. Within two years the idea of setting aside one day a year in tribute to mothers had swept the country, and the occasion has taken place every year since.

As first celebrated, Mother's Day was a solemn occasion, with church services being held and white carnations being distributed as a symbol of the purity of mother love.

Since those days the second Sunday in May has become a day of gift giving, with flowers playing an important part of the celebration as bouquets of bright spring flowers arrive at many a home from sons and daughters both far and near.

Flowers are also important for table decorations on Mother's Day, as family and friends gather for a festive dinner.

ROSES FOR MOTHER'S DAY

HERE are roses large and small to make for Mother's Day—tiny ones to trim pink candles and large ones for a bouquet.

To make the rosebuds, cut a strip of pink crepe paper about 2½" wide and 8" long. Cut across the grain so the edges of the buds can be slightly ruffled.

Fold the strip in half lengthwise and wind the folded strip, cut edges toward the stem, onto a small pipe cleaner. Wind tightly at first to make the center of the bud, and then gather the paper slightly as you go along. Dot the paper with stick glue as you wind. Then wind floral tape around the base of the rosebud and down about 2" of the stem. Snip off the excess pipe cleaner.

For a rosebud candle ring, make a 2" circle of 12-gauge wire. When you have 8 rosebuds, cut a leaf for each one of dark green paper and wind both leaves and buds onto the wire ring with strips of floral tape.

Wine glasses or goblets turned upside

down make excellent candlesticks. Secure the candle with floral clay, and slip the rosebud ring around the base of the candle.

Bouquet of Roses

Because Mother's Day comes in May and roses usually do not bloom until June, you can make your own bouquet for Mother with pink crepe paper.

Follow the same procedure as with the rosebuds. But this time make your strips longer and wider. Vary your strips so the roses will be of different sizes.

For stems, use 2 long pipe cleaners twisted together for extra length. Cut leaves of dark green crepe (or tissue) paper, and attach roses and leaves to the stems with floral tape. Give each rose 2 or 3 leaves.

Rosebud Nosegay

Tie a tiny nosegay to your Mother's Day gift, or make a full-sized one to use perhaps as a centerpiece.

For the small nosegay, make 6 rosebuds of different colors. Arrange them into a bouquet and twist the stems together, covering them with floral tape. For the collar use a 5″ paper lace doily. Make a slit to the center of the doily, and cut out a pie-shaped piece—about ¼ of the circle. Fasten the two cut edges together with glue to make a very wide cone shape, and slip the rosebud bouquet into the center. Tie a narrow satin ribbon around the stems and let the ends hang down several inches below the bouquet.

For a large nosegay, make larger roses and use a 9″ doily. The stems should be about 7″ long.

GIFT TRAYS

A LITTLE square pin tray, or a larger one for letters, lipsticks, or collections of earrings, can be made from the meat and poultry trays that you bring home from the market.

Wash the tray and let it dry. Then paint it with a bright fast-drying enamel, and decorate it with a cutout from a greeting card or with an illustration from a magazine. Secure the cutout with glue, and coat the entire tray, cutout and all, with clear lacquer. Be sure to coat it on both sides.

The trays are lightweight, colorful, and surprisingly sturdy. I've used my pin tray for several years.

EARLY AMERICAN
BANDBOXES

In the seventeenth and eighteenth centuries travelers carried their belongings, and particularly their finery, in large, colorful, cardboard or wooden boxes known as bandboxes. The forerunners of today's trunks and suitcases, they still make excellent containers for scarves, belts, handkerchiefs, and are very useful for packaging special gifts.

Bandboxes were originally made to hold men's collars and ruffs, which in those days were called "bands." This is how they were given the name of bandboxes.

Traditionally, these containers were covered with wallpaper and lined with newspaper. Small bandboxes, too, were fashionable, especially for ladies' wigs, caps, and laces. Most were fashioned in an oval shape; some were heart-shaped.

When ladies went to the theater in those days they would take off their bonnets and put on a dainty lace cap, called a cornet cap, which they had taken with them in a small bandbox. It just wasn't proper for ladies to be seen in public with their heads uncovered. The heart-shaped bandboxes were often used for the cornet caps.

Recently, bandboxes have become popular once more, along with the resurgence of all things antique. They are easy to make, very decorative, completely useful—and they make marvelous gifts.

To make a bandbox, start with a sheet of Bristol board and, if you plan to make a large one, say hat-box size, a sheet of 11-ply poster board. The poster board is sturdy and is excellent for the bottom and the cover. Both Bristol board and poster board are available in art-supply shops. Bristol board is usually sold in stationery stores as well.

For a medium-sized bandbox, one that will measure about 7" by 8½", and 6" tall, draw a rectangle on the poster board about 7" by 8½". Then round off the corners, as shown in the photograph, and cut out the bottom of the box. This gives you the traditional shape.

Measure the circumference—it will be about 26"—allowing an extra inch for the overlap, and cut out a strip of Bris-

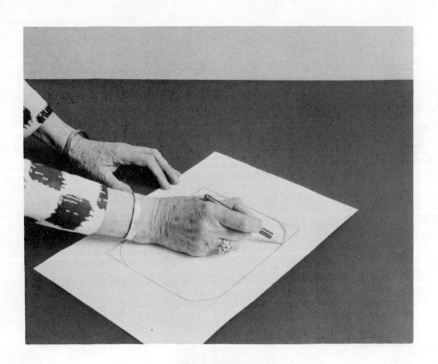

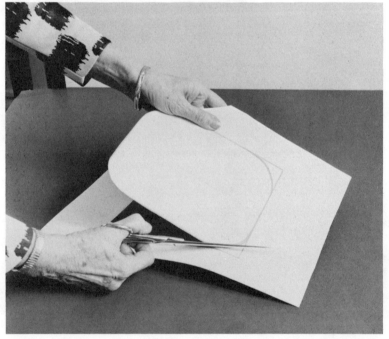

tol board for the sides of the box. It should be approximately 6″ wide and about 27″ long.

Along one edge, strip on masking tape, with half the tape exposed. Then roll the Bristol board around the bottom, pressing the masking tape to the bottom as you go. Overlap the sides by

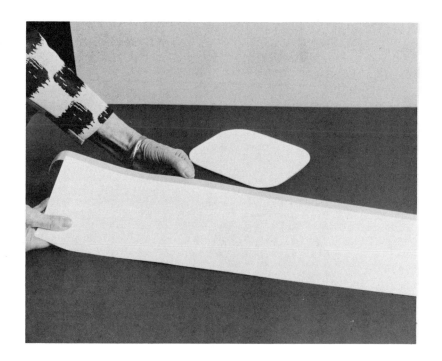

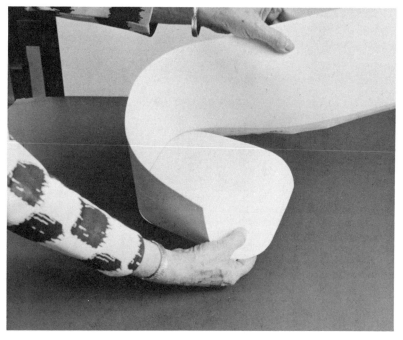

about 1″ and fasten them together by running a strip of masking tape up along the side of the bandbox.

To make the cover, draw around the box onto the poster board. The cover should be very slightly larger than the box, so it will slip on easily and yet be snug. Cut a strip of Bristol board about

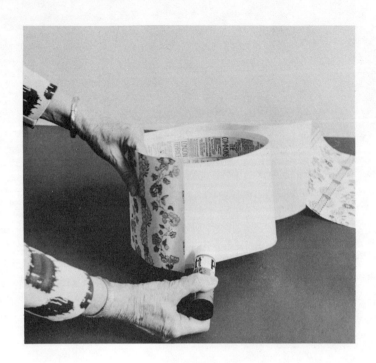

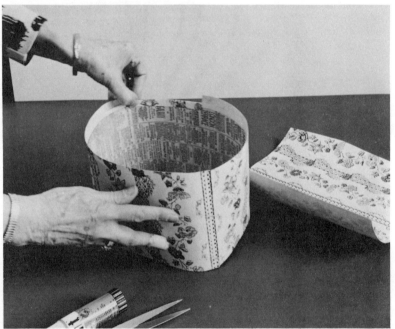

1½″ wide and 27″ long and attach this to the top, as you did the sides of the box to the bottom, using masking tape. This gives you a cover with sides 1½″ deep.

Traditionally, bandboxes were lined with newspaper since paper was scarce. The newspaper linings have served another purpose for us—they give a clue as to the age of antique bandboxes. I like

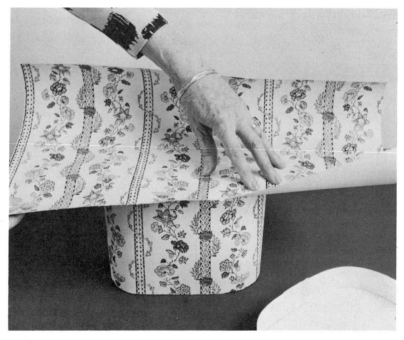

to line mine the same way, although for special birthday gifts and Mother's Day gifts it is nice to use colorful wrapping paper or flowered fabric. Use stick glue to attach the lining. It will not mar the paper as the white glues will do.

Many wallpaper concerns today reproduce the old designs of the wallpapers used in the eighteenth and early nineteenth centuries. These are exactly

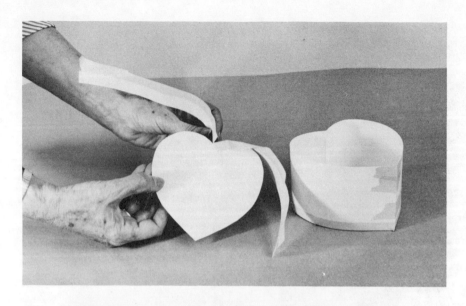

right for bandboxes if your aim is to be completely traditional. Otherwise, wallpapers of either scenic or colonial design will serve as covering very well.

To cover the sides of the box, cut a strip of wallpaper about 30″ long and 6½″ or 7″ wide. Attach with stick glue, leaving the extra ½″ or so at the top. When the sides are covered—and make sure you match the pattern where the two ends meet—snip around the top at

1″ intervals, fold down inside the box, and secure with stick glue. This will give the top edge of the box protection.

When you are ready to put the wallpaper on the cover, again keep in mind the pattern and match the design with that on the box itself. Cut the paper for the top of the cover large enough so it too can be snipped at 1″ intervals and folded down into the sides of the cover.

Finally, cut a strip of wallpaper 1½″

wide and about 30" long, using a part of the design that will make a decorative finish for the bandbox. Attach to the sides of the cover with stick glue.

To make the heart-shaped bandbox, proceed as with the oval shape; usually these are small—mine is about 4" across. Before you attach the sides to the heart-shaped bottom, fold the sides in half, strip masking tape along one edge as before, and start to attach the sides to the bottom at the top center of the heart, finishing at the point at the bottom. Snip off any excess Bristol board at the point of the heart, and fasten the sides together at the point with a small piece of masking tape.

THE TREASURE EGG

A DECORATED EGG for tiny treasures—to make as a gift or a party favor—starts with one of the plastic eggs used for hosiery containers. I painted the egg with a royal blue fast-drying enamel, glued a gold-colored cap from a small bottle on the top, trimmed the egg with gold braid around the top and middle, and glued it to a bottle cap for a stand. The stand too was painted royal blue.

For a fine Mother's Day gift, put a string of pearls or a pretty pin inside the brightly decorated egg.

Father's Day

Third Sunday in June

LIKE Mother's Day, Father's Day was first celebrated in 1908 in the state of West Virginia. This too is a time of gift giving and family gathering. In recent years it has expanded so that not only fathers are honored but grandfathers, uncles, and brothers. The Sunday dinner is a happy occasion, with more gifts than decorations the order of the day.

DESK SCREENS

SMALL screens have a thousand uses and make excellent gifts for Father's Day, as well as Mother's Day, and birthdays. And if you never want to throw away your handsomely designed calendars, here's the perfect solution—make them into screens.

Cut out your calendar (or other) pictures, and fold them into either 3 or 4 panels, depending on the width of the picture. If you want to keep the design completely intact, do not cut into panels. If your picture divides easily into separate sections, cut them into panels.

Cut out your picture, and then cut cardboard panels to fit the picture. Hinge these with straping tape—the kind that has thread running through it

—and secure your picture (or picture panels) to the cardboard panels with stick glue. You may have to pull the picture off and start again if you don't get it on straight the first time. The stick glue will let you do this.

Cover the back of your screen with panels cut from paper of small design and harmonizing color. These papers can be found in art shops, which usually have a wide assortment of colors and textures.

Edge the screen with colored cloth adhesive tape. It comes in many different colors and is usually about ⅝″ wide. Put this adhesive all around the screen, folding it over so half the width of the tape shows on both the back and the front of the screen.

If you have cut your picture into panels, strip the tape down between the

panels so the center of the tape is in the fold of the screen. If your picture runs right across the screen, strip the tape down between the panels on the back of the screen only.

My largest screen, cut from an Air India black-and-white calendar, is 12" by 15"; my smallest, which has only three panels and was cut from a Japanese calendar, is 8" by 11".

I have used my screens to hide the telephone, jars of paint brushes, and many other unsightly objects, including clusters of cosmetic containers in the powder room. And I've given screens to many friends upon request.

If after several months the tape should come loose, simply refasten it with white glue.

The screens are pretty, practical, and very long lasting.

DESK SET FOR FATHER

VERY useful and good looking too is a desk set that holds not only pencils but paper clips, scissors, paint brushes, pens, rubber bands, a ruler, and stamps.

Start with a sturdy piece of cardboard about 8½" by 11". A stiff corrugated cardboard works very well. Cut it into

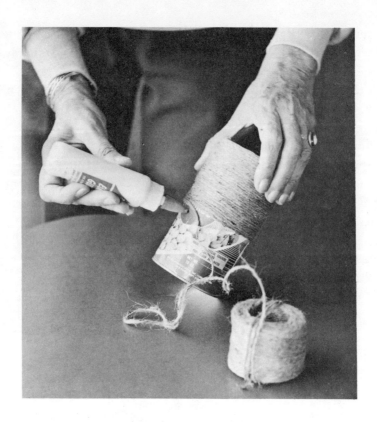

an oval shape, and paint it with a colorful fast-drying enamel, easier to keep clean than flat paint. (It is wiser to use a can of paint and a brush than a spray paint because you get fewer fumes.)

Choose 6 cans of varying sizes—save your soup cans, tuna fish cans, fruit cans, and whatever kinds might be suitable. Paint the insides of the cans with a paint to match the cardboard base.

Then wind rough-textured cord around the cans, securing with white glue as you go along. My cans vary in height from 1½" to 9", and from 1¼" to 3" across.

To finish off the tops of the containers, braid 6 strands of the cord together—2 strands to one of the 3 strips—and glue around the top. To finish the base, make another braid, this time using 6 strands of cord to each of the 3 pieces in the braid. Glue this around the base—it takes a braid about 32" long—and arrange the decorated containers on the base. When you have them placed as you want them, probably with the taller ones to the back, glue them to the base with white glue.

A medium blue paint and an oatmeal-colored cord make a good combination.

A variation of the corded set is one with cans painted with enamel, inside and out, and trimmed with colorful paper edgings cut from old greeting cards. The base of this one, painted to match the containers, is shaped around the cans, extending about a ½" beyond them. Glue the containers to the base with white glue.

Easter bunnies of pastel cardboard strips stand in groups or serve as place cards on the party buffet.

Easter place cards—flowers in flower pots—are bent at the bottom so they will stand up.

Easter baskets of ruffled crepe paper and shirred eyelet lace hold shredded grass and candy eggs.

A box to hold the Haggada booklets and an elegantly
trimmed felt matzah cover decorate a Seder table.

The maypole, May Day's popular symbol, becomes a
party centerpiece with dolls to hold the streamers.

Flowers for Mother's Day—
crepe paper roses in a yarn
trimmed bottle, and a ring
of rosebuds for the candle.

For a summertime children's party,
a crepe paper clown serves as
centerpiece and holds
a favor for each child.

For a simple summer
wedding, a bride and groom
with a cluster of bells
stand in front of a
three-panelled screen.

American Indian Day, celebrated in schools, is typified by a village with a wilderness background.

Bright feathers for the Indian Chief's headdress are cut from construction paper, glued to double headband.

The Sukkah, commemorating the Jewish harvest festival, is filled with the fruits of the field.

Fourth of July

INDEPENDENCE DAY is one of the best loved of American national holidays—the day on which we celebrate the nation's freedom from its political ties with Great Britain.

Although the actual breaking of those bonds occurred on July 2, it was on July 4, 1776, that the Continental Congress, meeting in Philadelphia with all thirteen colonies represented, officially adopted the Declaration of Independence. The Fourth has been celebrated ever since.

During the nineteenth century, the holiday was marked by patriotic speeches, parades, and fireworks, with flags flying from homes and public buildings. Picnics, too, were popular on the Fourth as families gathered together to commemorate the beginnings of the nation.

Early in the twentieth century, however, fireworks were banned in many cities and towns. They had caused so many fires and injuries that the hazards were considered to be greater than the beauty of the spectacle. The result is that most of the fireworks displays today are arranged by cities and towns for public celebrations.

Picnics and parades continue to be highlights of the patriotic celebration, with decorations carrying out the flag's red, white, and blue.

PATRIOTIC PARTY PIECE

A CENTERPIECE for a Fourth of July party should carry out the colors of our flag. Here's a red-white-and-blue arrangement that is suitable for an indoor buffet table or an outdoor picnic, and with a bit of prior preparation it can be assembled in minutes.

Start with 8 red apples, which will serve as candle holders, 7 white 5" candles and a white 10" candle. Around the base of each candle fasten a fringe of blue construction paper. This will both catch the the drips and help to wedge the candle into the apple. For the fringe cut a strip of blue construction paper 7" long and 2" wide, fringe one long side, and glue around the candle. Cut out the stems of the apples, making holes large enough to support the candles. Wedge the candles into the apples

with floral clay, and form a circle around the apple with the tall candle.

If you use the centerpiece outdoors on a windy day, leave the candles unlighted.

FOURTH OF JULY PARTY FAVORS

To brighten a patriotic party buffet, or to decorate a picnic table, make a set of favors that carry out the colors of the American flag.

Stand a tiny American flag—the kind that comes in a package of 12 and measures about 1" by ½"—in a large, red gumdrop. If you are using a fine linen tablecloth, protect it from the gumdrop by placing the favor on a circle of red paper. Make a favor for each guest and stand one at each place, or arrange a long line of gumdrops down the center of the table.

Summertime

THE warm and sunny days of summer are perfect for parties, which can be arranged indoors or out, as picnics or as barbecues or buffets, and the children, free from their school activities, can help make the decorations, especially when the parties are to celebrate their own birthdays.

Summer is the time when garden flowers and fresh greens can be gathered to trim a table or decorate a terrace, and the leisurely, informal atmosphere makes entertaining a pleasant part of the season.

WEDDING PARTY BUFFET

A BUFFET table for an informal wedding party can be decorated with the figures of a bride and groom and a string of wedding bells.

This bride is made of white felt, and she stands about 8″ tall. Make the body of a cardboard cone, using a third of a circle. Cover the cone with white felt, securing it with white glue. Snip off the top ¼″ of the cone.

The lady's head is a small cone—about a quarter of a 4″ circle—and this too is covered with white felt. It is then glued, point down, into the top of the body. Tie a piece of gold cord around the neck.

The bride's hat is a white felt ring, trimmed with gold cord. Follow the pattern given here. Glue the ends of the material together to form the ring, and glue this to the top of the head.

Cut the bride's cape out of white felt according to the pattern, trim it with gold braid, and glue it together at the center front. Slip it over the body.

Dip a few twigs and dried blossoms into gold paint and let them dry. Then form them into a bouquet, tie with black thread to hold them together, and glue the bouquet to the center of the cape, as though the bride holds them in her hands.

The groom is simpler to make. His body is a cone of black construction

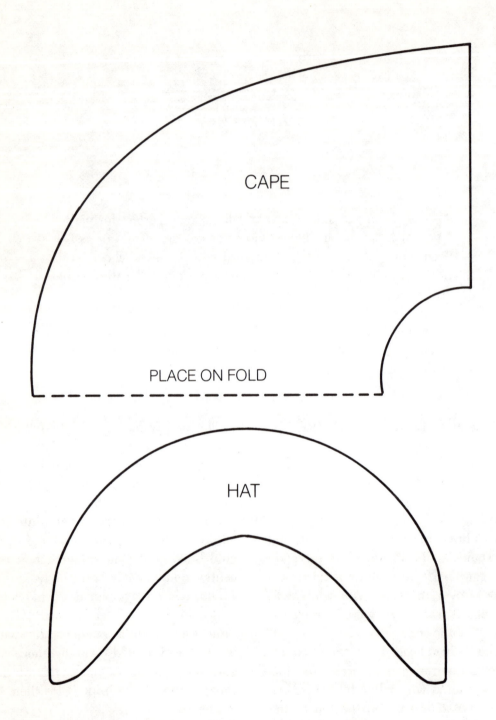

CAPE

PLACE ON FOLD

HAT

paper about 9″ tall. Snip off ¼″ at the top. The head is a small cone, about 2½″ tall (made from a quarter of a 5″ circle). I used white construction paper for the head. Glue it, point down, to the top of the body.

Three tiny white buttons, a bow tie, and a wing collar of white typing paper are pasted to the groom's black suit, attached with stick glue.

The groom's hat is a stovepipe made of a 2″ by 6″ strip of black construction paper. Glue the short edges together to form the stovepipe, and then glue that to an oval piece, about 2″ by 2½″, which will serve as the brim. Then secure the hat to the top of the head with stick glue.

I haven't given faces to my figures, but of course they can be drawn on with a felt pen if you like.

The string of wedding bells are made of white construction paper. Use half of a 4″ circle for each bell, and form into a cone. Fasten with stick glue. Trim the edges with gold cord.

To suspend the bell, cut a piece of matching cord about 8″ long, and tie a knot in one end. Slip the cord through the point of the cone and pull it through until the knot holds firm inside the bell.

Suspend the bells at different levels, and tie them to a gold satin bow.

If you want a background for your figures, make a 3-panel screen to stand behind them, and hang the bells on the screen.

I made my screen out of a 12″ by 18″ piece of cardboard. I folded it into 3 equal panels, and rounded off each panel at the top. Then I cut out the inside of each panel, leaving 1″ all around

as a frame. Next I painted the cardboard with gold paint—it needed two coats—and pasted gold braid around all edges.

I pasted red tissue paper on the wrong side of the screen to fill in the panels, to give the effect of stained glass. And in the center panel I added a pane of blue at the top. Then I hung the wedding bells on the screen and stood my figures in front of it for an effective buffet decoration.

THE INSTANT BIRTHDAY CAKE

THIS cake is good for an unplanned birthday party, or for any festive occasion when candles are called for. It is pretty, colorful, edible, and quick and very simple to make. In fact, you don't even have to make it—you just put it together.

On a flat cake plate place one large marshmallow for the center, circle it with a ring of marshmallows, and then another and another, until you have a circle of about 8″ across. This will take about 40 marshmallows—not quite a package.

On the center one place 2 more, making it the highest point of the "cake." Secure with toothpicks.

Then place one more on each of the marshmallows in the next ring, securing with toothpicks. Then place a candle holder on the center peak, which is 3 marshmallows high, and place holders along the outer ring—or more if you like. I usually use 14 or 15 candles, all in holders.

Around the "cake," place a circle of construction paper cutouts to match the color of the candles.

For the cake trim, cut 3 strips of construction paper 12″ long and 1½″ wide. Fold each strip in half, then in half again, and once more in half. This gives you 8 segments. Then cut a flower design in the folded construction paper strip, as shown in the drawing. When all 3 strips have been cut with the flower design, open them up, attach them together with Scotch tape to form a 36″ circle, and place the ring of flowers around the cake.

PLACE DOTTED LINES ON FOLDS

MARSHMALLOW PLACE CARDS

Marshmallow figures to hold place cards for a children's birthday party go very well with the "instant birthday cake." They are easy to make, colorful, and they delight young children.

Each figure is made of 3 large marshmallows, held together with toothpicks. The arms are made of 2 tiny marshmallows, also held together with toothpicks and secured to the body by toothpicks. If the toothpicks are too long, snip them off with scissors or simply break them off.

The peaked cap is a half circle of colored construction paper—each one a different color. The half circle, 4½" in diameter, is formed into a cone, and glued to the head with white glue. The place card, 1" by 1¾", matches the hat in color, with a smaller white card pasted to it on which to write the child's name. A ¼"-wide strip of matching construction paper serves as a handle, which is glued to the arm.

These marshmallow figures can be used again and again. The marshmallows will harden, and a new white card can be pasted to the place card for the next party's little guests.

THE PARTY CLOWN

A clown centerpiece for a children's party is always popular, especially when

the clown hides a little surprise package for each child.

Start with a plastic egg—the kind that is used as container for hosiery—and paste on it 2 oval black paper eyes and a red smiling mouth. Put a little rouge on his cheeks.

Make a cone-shaped hat of crepe paper, using about a quarter of a 14″ circle. This will give the clown a hat about 7″ tall. Cut a strip of paper of a contrasting color 2″ wide and about 12″ long; fringe the strip and roll it up into a tassle. Glue this to the peak of the hat. Glue the hat to the head.

Finish the hat with a 1″-wide brim. To make it, cut a 5″ circle of crepe paper, cut a 2″ circle out of the center, making a hole about 2″ across. Slip the brim over the peaked hat, and glue it in place with stick glue.

For the clown's collar, make a ring of silver paper (or any color, just as long as it is quite heavy), using a strip ½″ wide and 6″ long. Glue the short ends together to form a ring, and glue the clown's head into the collar with white glue.

Cut 6 circles of crepe paper—3 of one color and 3 of another—about 4½″ across. Cut holes in the center so the circles will fit over the collar. Glue them to the collar, alternating the colors, and ruffle the edges by gently stretching the paper.

The clown will sit on a bowl that holds tiny packages. Choose a mixing bowl that is about 8″ across; cut a round of cardboard for a cover, and glue onto it a dozen circles of crepe paper of the same alternating colors, and ruffle these edges gently. Then glue the clown's head, with his ruffled collar, to the cover.

Finally, cover the bowl with rows of colors. Use straight strips for these ruffles, and be sure to cut across the grain so the paper will stretch into ruffles.

When the clown is finished, fill the bowl with little favors wrapped in colorful paper. Tie a ribbon on each long enough to reach from the bowl along the table to each child's place.

MINIATURE HORSE
AND WAGON

MAKE use of the little treasures brought
home from your travels—combine them
with your own creations to give distinction to your party tables.

For a children's party table, a small
wagon pulled by a wooden horse from
Sweden and led by a little wooden
pojke (boy) makes an appealing scene.
Add a few large pine cones for a wood-
land effect.

For the wagon, cover an oblong box
with bright construction paper, and
glue a ribbon spool on each side for
wheels. Draw spokes on the wheels with
a felt pen.

Cut 2 strips of matching construction
paper for the harness, gluing one end of
each strip to the front of the wagon and
the other to a paper saddle. The saddle
is a strip of paper about 1″ wide and 4″
long. This will fit a horse about 6″ tall.

Place a little doll in the wagon—or
perhaps fill it with flowers.

A SWEDISH FAMILY
BIRTHDAY SETTING

In Sweden the birthday of a family member is an important event, and the celebration starts with breakfast.

A special cup and saucer, used only for birthdays, is set at the place of the member being honored and is circled by a garland of fresh flowers arranged on the tablecloth. The teapot, or coffeepot, is ready at hand, along with a gift in fancy wrapping, and the whole setting is surrounded by several vases of bouquets, forming a semicircle of flowers.

After the first ceremonial cup of tea or coffee, breakfast is served. And then the birthday cup and saucer are put back in the cupboard, to wait for the next member of the family to be feted.

American Indian Day

Fourth Friday in September

AMERICAN Indian Day, a holiday that honors the many tribes of native American Indians, is celebrated today by many states, usually on the fourth Friday of September. In some areas the date will vary, according to circumstances.

American Indians have had a great influence on our language and our geography, with such names as Massachusetts, Dakota, Illinois, and Connecticut. During this century the value and influence of these native Americans has been recognized. A day to honor them was established first in New York in 1912. Gradually the holiday has gained in popularity, until today, although it is not a national holiday, it is considered an important one, and one on which Indian traditions and lore are in evidence.

INDIAN VILLAGE

THE creating of an Indian village will bring all the lore of the Indian's world into focus for American Indian Day. Here's one version, simple enough for children to make.

Start with a setting in which to place your village. A colored photograph of a wilderness scene cut from a calendar or magazine will provide the backdrop. Cut out the picture, glue it to stiff cardboard, and put on "wings" if the scene is not large enough to encompass the whole village. I've used blue construction paper to extend my background.

Stand the backdrop on a large piece of light brown or sand-colored construction paper.

The village consists of as many tepees as you might like to make. For each, use about a third of a circle and form into a cone. Fasten with glue. To vary the height of your tepees, use a 16", a 14", and a 12" circle.

Cut off about 1" of the top of the tepee, and slip 3 or 4 poles—stems of dried weeds, or small trimmed branches —into the top opening. For a door, cut a

slit about 1½" long in the bottom of the cone, and fold back the flap. Use different shades of browns and tans for the tepees, as they were traditionally made of animal hides.

Place the tepees around a fire—represented by a pile of small stones—and add a miniature moose or elk, if you have them, to the scene.

The squaws sitting in my village are what the Indians call "pieces" dolls. They are made of scraps of material, quickly formed into dolls and given to Indian babies to stop their crying, according to an Indian I met in South Dakota. Here they sit in the village, waiting for the braves to come home from their hunting.

A totem pole, carved and painted to represent a spiritual ancestor of the tribe, stands at one side of the village.

THE TOTEM POLE

TOTEM POLES, which are symbolic of the Indians' spiritual ancestors, usually represent animals or birds. They are carved with grotesque features and painted in bright colors. Magic symbols too are sometimes included.

For a totem pole to stand in the Indian village, use a cardboard tube that comes with wax paper or aluminum foil. These are usually about 12" long.

Cover the tube with bright construction paper, and paint faces, feathers, and other Indian symbols on

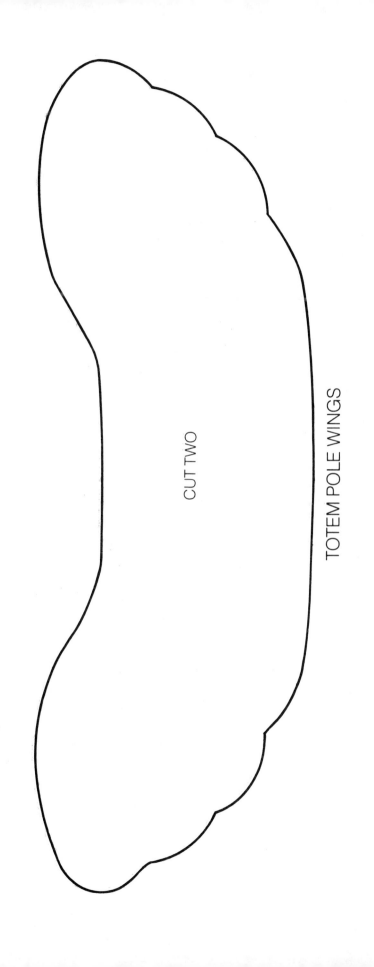

CUT TWO

TOTEM POLE WINGS

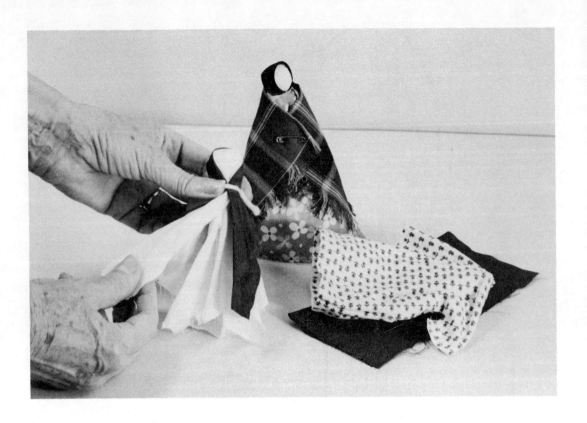

the pole. Cut a pair of cardboard wings with an 8″ wingspread, and paste to the pole near the top. Decorate the wings, too, painting feathers on them with bright-colored Magic Markers.

Pinch the top of the pole together to form a sort of head (an eagle's head, or an animal's head). Glue it together and cover with construction paper of a contrasting color.

To stand the pole up, glue it to a square base of corrugated cardboard.

THE PIECES DOLL

THESE traditional Indian dolls have no faces and are of different shapes and sizes, depending on how much fabric is available. For one of the right propor-

tion for your Indian village, start with a piece of white cloth about 6″ square. Shape it into a ball for the head. Over this, drape another square of white fabric, tie it at the neck, and let the rest fall easily for the body. Drape a piece of dark fabric over it, and tie at the neck.

The doll's calico dress is cut from a 3″ by 6″ piece of cloth. Cut it so there are sleeves, even though the doll has no arms, and tie at the waist. No edges are finished except for the hem of the dress, and this can be sewed or glued.

A cloak of dark fabric—a shawl made of a 6″ square folded in half—is wrapped around the doll's shoulders and fastened with a safety pin. Perhaps in the days before the safety pin the shawl was tied together.

INDIAN HEADDRESS

FEATHERS cut from construction paper of all colors are attached to a ribbon headband for an Indian Chief's headdress.

Cut the feathers about 10" long and 3" wide, and glue them between two layers of a 2"-wide ribbon or tape. Make the ribbons long enough so they can be used to tie on the headdress.

For an Indian maiden, use only 2 feathers of contrasting colors, and glue them to the back of the headdress.

Rosh Hashanah

September–October

(FIRST DAY OF THE LUNAR MONTH OF TISHRI)

Rosh Hashanah, the Jewish New Year, is celebrated by Jews everywhere. Observed for one day by Reformed and Conservative Jews, for two days by the Orthodox, it represents the new beginning, not only of the year but also of the world, the renewal of life and the reaffirming of faith. It is the day when the ram's horn—the shofar—is sounded, signifying God's supremacy and his judging of all men. It is also the first day of Tishri, a month in the Jewish calendar that has two other important holidays—Yom Kippur, the Day of Atonement, and Sukkot, the Festival of the Harvest.

During the observance of Rosh Hashanah, a ceremony that takes place in the synagogue, the shofar is sounded three times: once in praise of God, once as a memoriam, and a last time to announce the coming of important events.

Traditionally, in the afternoon some Orthodox Jews gather at the waterside, if there is water nearby, to cast out their sins, symbolically tossing them to the waves as a beginning of the ten days of penitence that follow.

One of the customs of Rosh Hashanah is the sending of greeting cards to friends and relatives to wish them a happy New Year and a prosperous year ahead. The ram's horn is an important symbol of the holiday, of course, and since this is one time when the ceremony takes place in the synagogue rather than at home, school children sometimes create a temple, suggesting the scene of the celebrating of this important occasion.

Yom Kippur

September–October

Yom kippur is the culmination of the ten days known as the High Holidays, the final emerging from the old year and its sins, and the day when the New Year, with its hopes and promises, is fully proclaimed. It is also the day when fasting is decreed, completing the purging of sins of the year past.

This is the most solemn day of the Jewish year, when all sins have been atoned for and all people are cleansed and ready for whatever comes in the New Year. From sundown the evening before until sundown on Yom Kippur, nothing is eaten. Many Jews do not even take water until the holiday is over.

During the Yom Kippur ceremony, the most impressive moment comes with the singing of the "Kol Nidre," a hauntingly beautiful chant whose words both admonish the worshippers to be particularly cautious in the making of personal vows before God and release them from the guilt of profaning God's name if they indeed fail to keep such vows. The "Kol Nidre" applies only to vows an individual makes to God himself, and in no way affects his obligations to others.

With the final sounding of the shofar, the Day of Atonement is over, and evening prayers begin.

Sukkot

September–October

(FIFTEENTH DAY OF THE LUNAR MONTH OF TISHRI)

SUKKOT is the annual Festival of the Harvest, a celebration that lasts for eight days. It begins on the fifteenth day of Tishri, the seventh month of the Jewish calendar—a month that starts with Rosh Hashanah—and commemorates both the harvest of the year past and the renewing of all life for the seasons ahead.

This is the time when the Jewish people build open shelters under the stars—sukkah—and decorate them with the crops of the fields, with fruits, vegetables, branches, and shrubs. These little structures symbolize the time of the harvest and the journey out of Egypt when the people had to live in temporary shelters.

In ancient days Jews probably lived in the sukkah while they gathered in the crops. Later on the custom took on historical significance, representing the difficulties the Jews found as they left Egypt. The custom of building a sukkah is still followed today in some areas, although, particularly in the cities, the building of the little structures has become a purely symbolic event. School children create their own little models, and the synagogues construct booths and fill them with the fruits of the harvest.

THE SUKKAH

THE little shelter known as the Sukkah can be made in various ways. One of the most popular is to build it in a shoe box. For the one shown here I used a shoe box cover as a trellislike frame, with openings so the sky and stars will shine through. The four sides are open.

Cut out 2 square openings, each 4″ by 4″, in the cover, leaving a center strip and a strip around the four sides of the top. In each corner of the cover, glue a cardboard pillar to hold up the trellis. For each pillar cut a piece of corrugated cardboard 7″ long and 2″ wide. Fold in half lengthwise for added strength.

Cover the pillars with stems of dried weeds of various kinds, fastening them with Titebond Glue. Tie bunches of dried plants to the pillars—use very thin wire or dark thread. Trim the trellis with straw or other dried foliage. If you have a little wooden bird, perch it on a corner of the trellis.

The Sukkah was intended to be lived in for the eight days of the holiday, and so there should be a table filled with food, and people to "live" in the shelter.

The table in my Sukkah is made from a box 4½" long, 2¼" wide, and 2" deep. Cut out the sides of the box, leaving ½" legs at each corner. To give an old look to the table, I painted mine with brown acrylic paint, and then daubed it with white paint.

On the table I put a miniature iron pot filled with dried beans, a tiny pottery pitcher, a wooden mug, and a copper jug. Any very small utensils will do.

The father, who is coming into the Sukkoth followed by the lamb, is a clothespin doll mounted on cardboard. The mother feeding the chickens is a hickory nut doll. The family's donkeys stand nearby.

Any little figures and animals that you might have in your collection will bring your Sukkah to life.

THE CLOTHESPIN DOLL

A WOODEN clothespin is used for this traditional doll from the days of colonial America. With a sharp ball-point pen,

draw a face on the rounded top of the clothespin. Next, make 2 tubelike black trouser legs, using pieces of material 2½″ long and 2″ wide. Glue the fabric into tubes, and slip them onto the clothespin, securing them with glue. Add a strip about ¾″ wide for the waist. Glue in place.

For the arms, glue a 4″ piece of pipe cleaner to the back of the doll's neck. Cover this with red fabric, glued on, and bend one hand to hold a walking stick of dried weed stem or a twig. Glue on cotton batting for the hair and beard, and finish off the doll with a cone-shaped hat made of black fabric. Form the cone with three quarters of a circle 1½″ in diameter. Glue to the doll's head.

To make the doll stand up, cut 2 oval-shaped pieces of corrugated cardboard, make a slit in the oval pieces large enough for the ends of the clothespin to slip into, and glue on the "feet." Cover with black acrylic paint, or color with a black Magic Marker.

THE LITTLE NUT-HEAD DOLL

THE little lady who wears a red babushka has a small nut for a head. A hazel nut is about the right size. With a sharp ball-point pen, draw eyes—tiny dots with fine lines over them for eyebrows—a dot for the nose, and a tiny curved line for a smiling mouth. Use the pointed end of the nut for the face—the point becomes the nose.

Glue a few loops of gray yarn to the top of the nut, and wrap the head with a piece of red fabric 2″ wide and 8″ long. Fasten it to the head with glue, and tie the neck with thread.

For the top of the body, drape the rest of the red fabric over another, larger, nut—a hickory nut is about the right size—and tie the waist with thread. Make an underskirt of stiff material, cutting it 3″ wide and 5″ long. Gather the skirt around the waist and fasten by sewing or with glue. Glue a piece of pipe cleaner about 5″ long across the shoulders of the doll for arms.

Dress the doll in a calico that has a very small print—she stands only about 5″ tall and a large print would not be suitable. Cover the stiff underskirt with the calico. Cut the material the same size as for the stiff underskirt, and gather at the waist. Then cover the bodice and arms, and tie the wrists with thread.

Cut a 4″ square of the red fabric with pinking shears so the edges won't have to be finished, and fold it to form a triangle. Drape it around the doll's shoulders, and make a little white apron for her.

If you want to give her a basket, use the cap of a large acorn or a half of a walnut shell. Glue a fine wire to the inside of the shell for a handle, and put a scrap of calico into the basket to protect the eggs, or whatever she is carrying. And place her in your Sukkah.

Columbus Day

October 12

COLUMBUS DAY is celebrated on October 12 not only in the United States but in Central and South America, in Spain, Italy, and Canada. It is the anniversary of the date on which Christopher Columbus landed in America—October 12, 1492—after two and a half months at sea, searching for a passage to China.

Cristoforo Columbo was born in Genoa, Italy, went to sea when he was a child, and decided while still in his twenties to try to find the mysterious country of China by sailing westward instead of eastward, as was usual at the time.

On August 3, 1492, with the sponsorship of the King and Queen of Spain, Columbus set sail westward with three ships—the *Santa Maria,* the *Pinta,* and the *Nina*—not knowing where the route would lead him.

Nine long weeks after sailing toward the setting sun, Columbus came to an island that he named San Salvador. Being sure he had found the Orient, he named the natives Indians. That speck of land, it is thought today, was probably the tiny Watling Island, southeast of Nassau in the Bahamas.

Columbus Day was first celebrated in New York on October 12, 1792, and not again, as far as we know, for one hundred years. On October 12, 1893, at Chicago's World Columbian Exposition, President Benjamin Harrison proclaimed Columbus Day as a general holiday.

In 1937 President Franklin Roosevelt designated each Columbus Day to be "observed with appropriate ceremonies in schools, churches, and other suitable places."

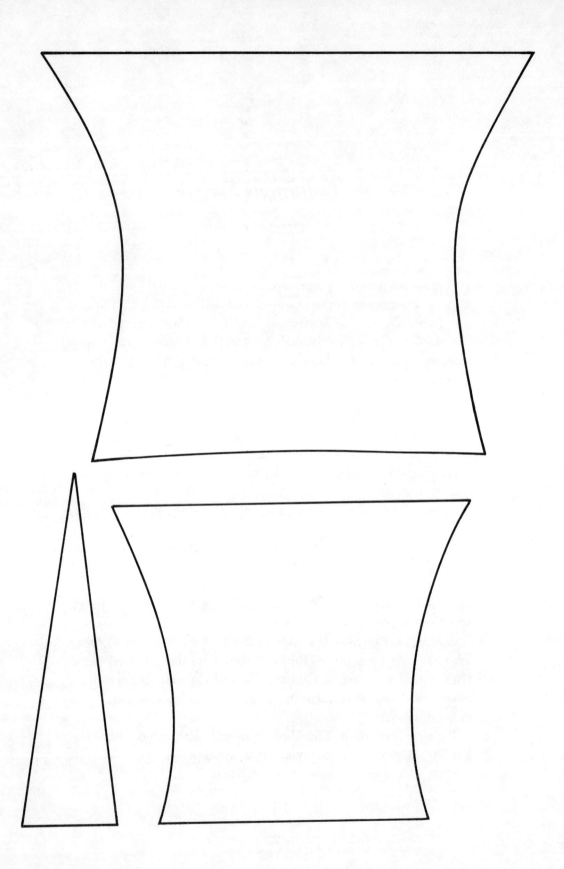

Parades are usual on Columbus Day all across America, with flags flying and bands playing—a joyous occasion in honor of the navigator who first found the lands on the western side of the Atlantic.

COLUMBUS DAY SHIP

QUICK and easy to make is the paper sailing ship for a buffet party centerpiece. It has three colors—red, white, and blue—and if you want to complete the fleet, you can make three ships, each one smaller than the next.

Start with a small cardboard box—mine is 2¼" by 3", and 1" deep—as a base for the ship. Fill the box with sand or pebbles.

Next cut out the sides of the ship, using blue construction paper and following the design given here. My ship is 12" long, 5½" high at the prow, and 4½" high at the stern.

Cut narrow ships of white construction paper to trim the sides of the ship, shaping the strips to fit the curve of the vessel. Where the deck supposedly is raised near the prow, paste on a straight strip of white to indicate

the lift, and finish the trim along the prow. Use stick glue—it holds well and will not mar the paper.

Glue the two sides of the ship together at the front and back edges. Then glue the box inside the boat, making sure it is at about midpoint.

For the mast, stand a plastic drinking straw in the box of pebbles. If the straw isn't long enough, cut a piece of another straw, crimp the end a little, and fit it into the top of the first straw. My mast, with its extension, is 14" tall.

To make 2 sails, cut each pattern twice, and glue each pair together around the mast, with a dab of glue on the mast to hold the pieces in place. White construction paper works best for these sails.

To finish off the little ship, glue a red paper triangle to a toothpick, and insert the toothpick into the top of the mast, securing it with a bit of floral clay.

United Nations Day

October 24

IT was on October 24, 1945, that the United Nations Charter was accepted by the majority of member nations which were meeting in San Francisco. Two years later, in 1947, President Harry S Truman proclaimed October 24 as United Nations Day. Since then, each year the President of the United States has decreed that October 24 be observed as United Nations Day, for the purpose of expanding everyone's awareness of the goals and accomplishments of the world organization.

The holiday is celebrated in schools and public buildings such as libraries and town halls with displays featuring information about foreign countries, displays of maps, flags, pictures, and crafts, in an effort to expand the horizons and increase the knowledge of students and others about how people of other nations live. With such displays, both at school and at home, the day of observation emphasizes the UN's attempts toward peace around the world.

DOLLS OF THE NATIONS

ONE OF the nicest ways to commemorate United Nations Day is to arrange a display of dolls of many nations. If you plan to decorate a mantel or a table at home, combine your dolls in groups or stand them in a row. You'll have a colorful arrangement even with only a few of the countries represented. Remember to include little dolls as well as the big, beautifully costumed foreign ones. If you have an Indian doll, or a little cornhusk doll, put these in your display —they too represent the peoples of the world.

If an arrangement of dolls is to be a classroom project, the display will be a large one. Bring whatever foreign dolls you have at home, tie a little tag to each one with your name on it so you won't forget which ones are yours, and to-

gether with your classmates, make a distinguished display.

Some dolls will be large, some small. To make a stage set of different levels for them to stand or sit on, use boxes of various sizes. Cover the boxes with construction paper, using the same color for all of them so they won't detract from the colorful costumes of the dolls.

I used 8 boxes for my display and covered them with a pale yellow paper.

I've included little ceramic dolls from Norway and Russia, wooden ones from Sweden. The large German doll in her dark pinafore is carrying a basket of flowers; the lady from Turkey has her long-haired goat with her; and the fisherman in white from the Island of Madeira stands proudly beside the red-garbed flower lady from the same island. There is a tall black native from the Continent of Africa, and dolls from

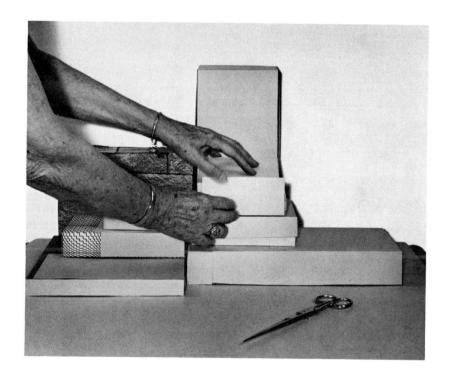

China and Japan. And America is represented by great-grandmother's doll, with two American Indian dolls standing nearby.

FLAGS OF THE WORLD

PACKAGES of small flags of all nations are available at stationery shops and art-supply stores. They are mounted on toothpicks, and when secured into a large red apple they make a symbolic world of nations.

Choose the largest apple you can find, making sure it has a strong stem so it can be suspended by a thread. Polish it and then insert the flags. Hang the apple over your doll display or suspend it in a hallway or window.

For a buffet table decoration, place a large grapefruit on a tray, and cover the grapefruit with the colorful flags.

Halloween

October 31

ALTHOUGH the custom of dressing up in fearsome costumes and masks to ward off evil spirits dates from pagan times, it was in the eighth century that Pope Gregory IV proclaimed November 1 as All Hallows Day, or All Saints' Day, to commemorate the saints who had died. Thus, the evening before, October 31, came to be known as All Hallow's Even, or Halloween, and traditionally it has been a time when it was thought that witches and ghosts roamed the earth, a night to be wary of these wicked creatures and mischievous elves.

In modern times, Halloween has become a night of great excitement for the children. They dress up in colorful costumes and masks, and go through the neighborhood ringing doorbells and demanding a "treat" in exhange for protection from a "trick." Apples, nuts, and candy are offered to appease these "witches," and off the children go to the next house.

During the past decade children on Halloween have begun carrying UNICEF boxes, asking for pennies for the United Nations Children's Fund, along with the usual fruit and candy. The schools gather up these coins and add them to the funds that provide food and care for needy children around the world.

Halloween parties are popular today for both children and grown-ups. Guests come in costumes and masks, and the festivities include prizes for the best outfit, ducking for apples, dancing, and, of course, enjoying all kinds of goodies from a decorated and laden buffet table.

WELCOMING PARTY GHOST

A GHOST to welcome your Halloween party guests is easy to make. Stand it by the front door or in the entrance hall.

A tripod makes a fine structure on which to build your ghost. Extend it as high as it will go. Over the top tie a large round clump of cotton batting or Poly-fil for the head. Over this, drape a white sheet, tie it around the neck with a black necktie, and paste black construction-paper eyes, nose, and mouth onto the face. A coat hanger forms the shoulders.

Give your ghost a witch's hat. Make a tall cone of black construction paper, using about a third of a circle. For the brim, cut an oval about 9″ by 12″ in size. Cut a hole in the center so it will fit over the ghost's head, and glue the cone securely to it.

If you don't have a tripod, use an artist's easel, or a floor lamp with its bulb and shade removed.

HALLOWEEN PLACE SETTING

PUMPKIN place mats give color to a Halloween party table, and they can also be

used for an informal Thanksgiving luncheon.

Cut a pumpkin shape out of newspaper, experimenting until you have the design you want, and use this for your pattern. Make the pumpkin about 10" high (without the stem) and about 14" wide.

First, cut out a pumpkin of orange felt, and then cut one of burlap, making the burlap one about an inch smaller all around so the orange will show at the edges. Fasten the two pieces together, burlap on top, with a few drops of glue.

Cover both sides of the place mat with transparent Contact, which is self-adhesive. This will give protection to your table and make the mats reusable.

To complete your table setting, trim the plastic top of a one-pound coffee can for a coaster. Cut circles of felt and burlap and glue them to the inside of the coaster. Glue orange bias binding around the outside edge, and put one ring of heavy orange (or brown) yarn inside the edge to hide the plastic.

For individual candleholders, cover small tuna fish cans with burlap. Wind a double ruff of orange paper around the base of an 8" candle, and fasten it in the can with floral clay.

HALLOWEEN TROLL

To SET the mood for Halloween, make a kindly troll of burlap and calico. She will give color to your Trick-or-Treat table.

Trolls are second-cousins of witches, and they live in the mountains of Norway, only venturing forth from their caves on nights when witches are abroad.

Start with a piece of 12-gauge wire about 35" long. Make a loop 6" long for one leg, twisting the wire together at the "waist." Without cutting the wire, make a second loop 6" long for the other leg, and twist at the top.

Again without cutting the wire, make loops for the arms, each loop about 4" long.

Find a large, well-wrinkled English walnut for the head. Fasten it to the body frame by winding masking tape around it. Keep the seam of the nut for the face—the seam makes the nose. Cover the head with long white yarn for hair, and with a felt pen draw eyes, eyebrows, a mouth, and two tiny dots for the nose, one on each side of the seam.

Tie a burlap skirt around the body. Make it a full skirt, and long enough to almost cover the feet.

Glue oblong-shaped pieces of black felt to the wire feet, orange felt to the hands, and pin a calico shawl over the troll's head and shoulders. Cut a piece 6" square, and fold it into a triangle.

If you have a piece of dried grass or a few twigs, give the troll a broom. Bend the wire legs so she will sit down, and put her in charge of the tricks and treats.

HALLOWEEN WITCH

DECORATE your doorway for Halloween with a witch, or hang her in a hallway where she will "fly" with every breeze.

Make the witch's body like the troll's, but make it larger. From her neck to her toes, the witch is about 8" long. Her arms are 5" long, including the hands. Use 12-gauge iron wire, as with the troll.

Attach a walnut head to the wire body with masking tape, and make use of the seam of the nut for the nose. Draw on large eyes and eyebrows and a mouth, and make two small dots for the nose. Glue long strands of white yarn to the head for hair.

Tie a full skirt of orange felt around the waist, and make it long enough to almost cover the feet. Glue pieces of orange felt to the feet and top them with slightly smaller pieces of dark green felt

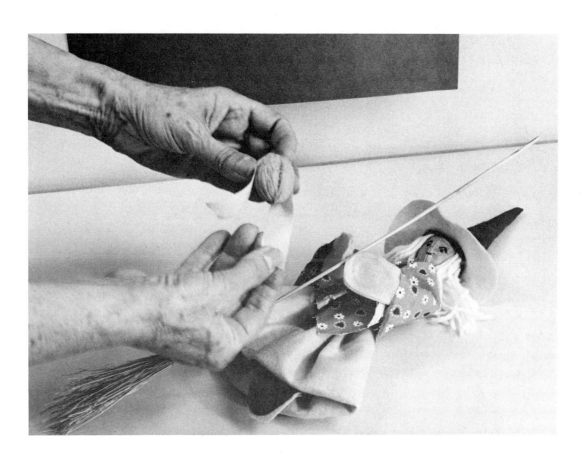

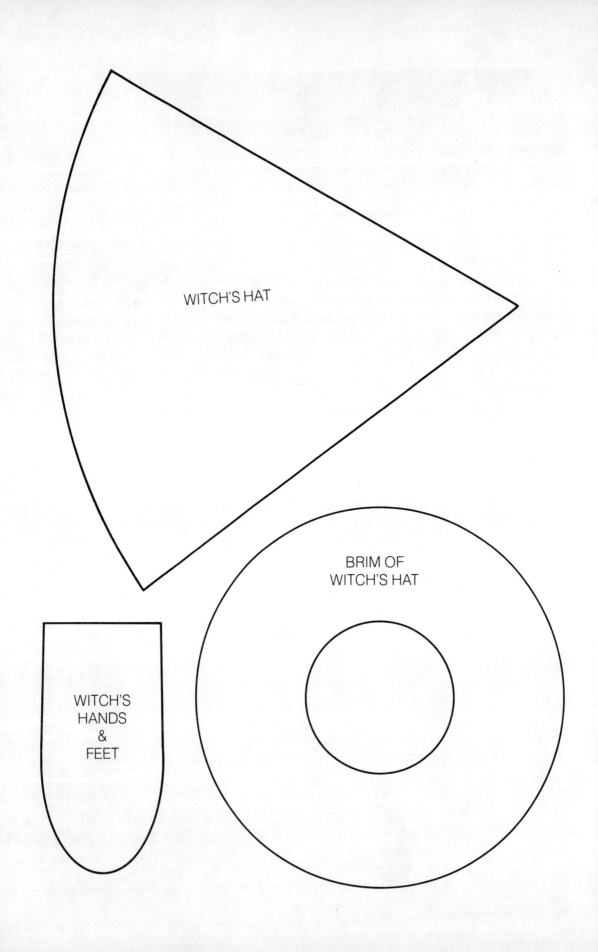

WITCH'S HAT

BRIM OF
WITCH'S HAT

WITCH'S
HANDS
&
FEET

for her shoes. Make her hands of orange felt—two pieces glued together.

Give the witch a calico shawl—a 9″ square folded into a triangle. This will cover the wire body and arms.

For the witch's hat, use dark green felt trimmed with an orange felt brim. Cut the pieces according to the patterns given. Form the cone-shaped hat and secure it with glue; then glue it to the head. Slip the orange brim over it, and fasten it in place with a touch of glue.

A witch always needs a broom. I used a stalk of dried glass for the handle and tied several snips of broom straw to it. Make the broom quite long—mine is 16″ long—so it will extend beyond her feet when she holds it in her hands.

Attach black thread to the back of the witch's head if you want to hang her up. You can, of course, tie the thread to the peak of the hat, but if you fasten it to the neck she will tip forward a little as though she were flying.

HOLIDAY CANDLESTICK

SOMETIMES when we are arranging our holiday buffet tables we find that we need just one or two more candlesticks— or perhaps we need candlesticks that will go with our color scheme. Here's one that is easy to make, with materials that you probably have at hand.

Cover a small can (8 oz.) with felt of the color you want. White glue will hold it. On the top of the can glue a 35mm film container—the little can that we always just toss away. Make sure the open end is up. This is also covered with felt of the same color.

Secure your candle in the candlestick with floral clay. Trim the bottom, the middle and the top with small pine cones. Glue them in place with white glue or Titebond.

Thanksgiving Day

Fourth Thursday in November

HARVEST festivals have taken place for as long as crops have been grown, with the celebrations in pagan days being conducted to honor the various goddesses of the fruits of the earth.

Our own Thanksgiving Day dates back to 1621, when the Pilgrims in Plymouth, Massachusetts, having weathered their first winter in the New World and successfully harvested their first crops, declared a day of thanksgiving to celebrate the great accomplishment. They invited the friendly Indian chief, Massasoit, who came with ninety of his braves, and together they enjoyed a feast of venison, fowl, fish, corn, and various kinds of greens, with berries and fruits for dessert.

Through the years a day of thanksgiving was occasionally celebrated in America, but without any regularity and at different times in different places. Finally, in 1863 President Abraham Lincoln proclaimed the fourth Thursday of November as Thanksgiving Day. Some, but not all, of the Presidents who followed him declared a day of thanksgiving in the fall, but it was not until 1942 that, by Congressional order, the fourth Thursday in November was named as Thanksgiving Day, to be observed as a national holiday.

Traditionally, Thanksgiving is a time for families to gather together for a dinner of turkey, cranberry sauce, and several kinds of vegetables, to be topped off with pumpkin or squash pie. It is a time of party giving and the exchanging of greetings with friends, and in recent years it has become the day on which many parades are held to announce the Christmas season.

FRUIT PYRAMID
FOR THANKSGIVING

A BOUNTIFUL pyramid of fruits and nuts
—edible, colorful, and traditional—can
decorate your dinner table even though
you do not have a series of stemmed
fruit dishes to stack together.

Start with a round tray. I used one
about 11″ in diameter. On this I put a
stemmed compote (the only one I
have), which is 5½″ tall and 9″ across.
Next, I inverted a small bowl on the
compote and put a 7″ plate on that. I
topped the pyramid with a sherbet
glass, which was just large enough to
hold a pear.

Arranging the apples, grapes, ba-
nanas, and other fruits was simple once
I had my structure completed, and all
the little gaps between the fruits were
filled in with mixed nuts.

PINE-CONE TURKEYS

A FLOCK of pine-cone turkeys will trim
a Thanksgiving table, surround a centerpiece of fruit, run down the length of

a Thanksgiving buffet table, or act as carriers of place cards for the guests at a traditional turkey dinner.

Choose pine cones about 3½" or 4" high. For the tail use tissue paper in various shades of orange and brown. If you can't find the multicolored paper, use orange. Cut a half circle about 7" across, and fold it into ½" accordion pleats. Insert the folded paper into the pine scales at about the midpoint of the cone, and secure with a drop of glue. Fan out the tail.

For the beak, use orange construction paper. Cut a quarter of a 4" circle, form into a narrow cone, and slip the "beak" over one of the scales. Fasten with a spot of glue. Bend down about 1" of the point of the beak.

If you want to use your turkeys for place cards, write your guest's name on a small white card and glue it to the creature's beak.

COPPER LANTERN

FOR a warm glow on the Thanksgiving dinner table, there's nothing that can match a copper lantern. Most craft shops sell sheets or rolls of copper, and it is easy to cut with ordinary scissors.

I made my copper lantern 3" square and 6" high. First, make a pattern on newspaper, as shown in the drawing, and trace the pattern onto the copper sheet with a soft pencil.

Cut out the lantern and fold on the dotted lines. This will give you a square with all sides rounded at the top. Secure with Scotch tape on the outside of the lantern. This seam will be at the back

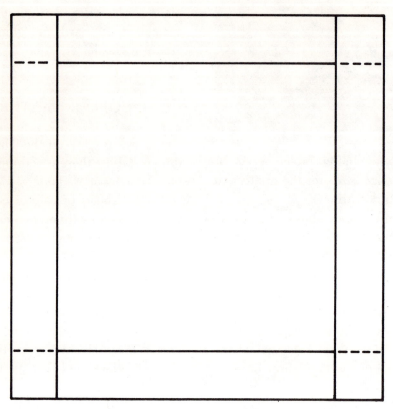

CUT ON DOTTED LINES—FOLD ON ALL LINES

and will be covered later with strips of gold braid.

With small scissors (manicure scissors work well) cut out the face of the lantern, leaving a ½″ frame all around. Trim all edges of the opening with self-adhesive gold braid, and put gold braid around each of the four sides of the copper lantern.

For the candle tray, which is entirely separate, cut a 3½″ square of copper, and fold up the sides so the tray will just fit inside the lantern. Then fasten a candle to the tray with floral clay—or with melted wax—and light the candle. Your lantern will be safe, and you will love the copper glow.

Halloween troll, made of wire,
burlap and calico, has a walnut head.
Her "broom" is a dried weed.

The Halloween witch flys on her
broomstick from a hall doorway.
Her head is a wrinkled walnut.

A bountiful centerpiece for
Thanksgiving combines fruits and
nuts, symbolic of the harvest.

Pinecone turkeys, with tails of
pleated tissue paper, hold
place cards in their beaks.

An Advent Calendar is trimmed with cutouts from
last year's greeting and Christmas cards.

Hanukkah gifts done up
in hand-decorated wrappings
bring color to the
family holiday scene.

The Christmas crèche—cardboard wound with rough cord,
has figures made of construction-paper cones.

For a Christmas village, cover cans with paper and
glue on cones for the tops of the towers.

Bandboxes covered with wallpaper are useful and
decorative gifts. See Mother's Day section for details.

Christmas trees made of lace and glued to plain
cards create old-fashioned season's greetings.

COPPER LANTERN

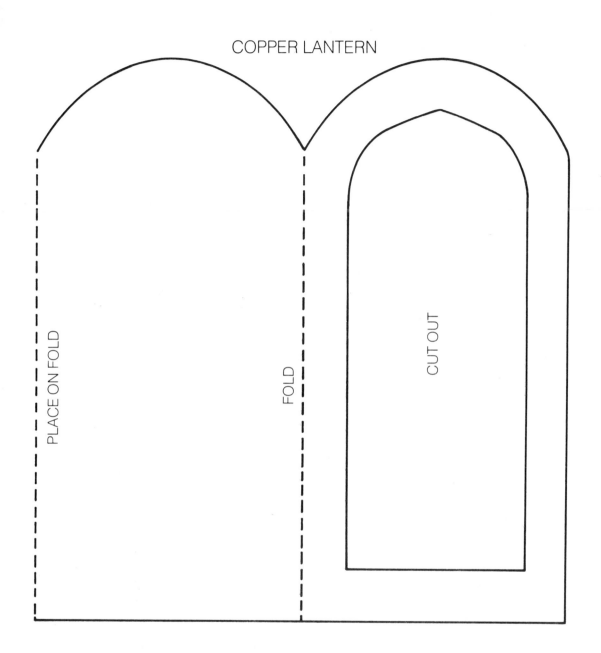

PLACE ON FOLD

FOLD

CUT OUT

Hanukkah

November–December

(25TH DAY OF THE LUNAR MONTH OF KISLEV)

Back in the second century B.C. the Jewish Temple of Jerusalem was taken over by the Syrian King Antiochus in his struggle against the Egyptians for the land of Palestine. In his desire to establish religious conformity in his conquered lands, he tore down the Jewish altar, decreed that it would henceforth become a temple to the Greek god Zeus, and forbade the observing of religious rituals by the Jews.

A group of Orthodox Jews rebelled, fled to the hills to arm themselves, and with Judah the Maccabee in command, defeated Antiochus's forces. They recaptured the Temple and proclaimed a celebration of rededication that would last for eight days.

This celebration came to be known as Hanukkah, which in Hebrew means "dedication." Not only is it a celebration of a military victory; it symbolizes the rededication of the religious beliefs of the Jewish people.

Hanukkah is called the Festival of Lights. Eight candles are placed in the menorah, and one is lighted each night for eight nights. The story is told that when the Maccabees tried to relight the sacred lamp in the Temple of Jerusalem, they found only enough oil for one night. By a divine miracle, the oil burned for eight nights—and thus the custom has been carried on.

Hanukkah is a happy holiday, a time of gift giving and game playing for children as well as adults. Greeting cards are exchanged, special foods are prepared—such as the potato *latkes* or pancakes—and homes are decorated.

THE MENORAH

THE menorah, the traditional candle that is used at Hanukkah time, is made up of eight candleholders—one candle for each day of the holiday, and one extra with which to light the others. At other festivals of the Jewish year a seven-branched menorah is used, symbolizing the seven days of creation. Only at Hanukkah is the eight-branched menorah used.

Menorahs are made in many different designs and with different materials, from brass to silver and from glass to pottery. Here are two ways to put a menorah together. The first one uses wine glasses (or goblets) turned upside down. With the tallest glass in the center for the lighting candle, match as well as you can the four pairs that make up the rest of the arrangement. Mine are not matched exactly, but they are similar in size and shape.

For the large center candle, I use a 5″ one; for the others a 4″ candle is about right. Secure them to the glasses with floral clay, and trim the base of each candle with tiny pine cones or dried seed pods to cover the clay.

Another style of menorah, this one more colorful, can be made with eight soup cans and one taller can. Cover the cans with bright blue crepe paper, and trim the tops with gold braid. (Use stick glue with the crepe paper—the white glues will mar it.)

Secure a votive candle to the top of each candleholder, using floral clay. The bottoms of these candles are not always completely flat—use clay to make them stand straight. Arrange them with the tallest candleholder in the center.

THE DREIDEL

ONE OF the games the children enjoy at Hanukkah is played with a dreidel—a four-sided top that has a different Hebrew letter on each side. According to which letter comes up when the top stops spinning, the player either takes part of a kitty of nuts and raisins or pays a forfeit.

To make a dreidel, start with a cardboard box 2″ square. Cut the cardboard according the pattern given, and tape the edges together. Cut a small hole—slightly smaller than the handle you plan to use, so it will fit snugly—through the center of top and bottom of the box. Cover the box with colored paper, and cut openings in top and bottom to match those in the box. Paste a cutout of a Hebrew symbol (see pat-

terns) on each side of the dreidel, and insert the stem.

A ¼″ dowel about 4″ long and sharpened at one end in a pencil sharpener is best for the stem, but a pencil or ballpoint pen can also be used. Let the point extend no more than 1″, which will leave 1½″ at the top for the handle.

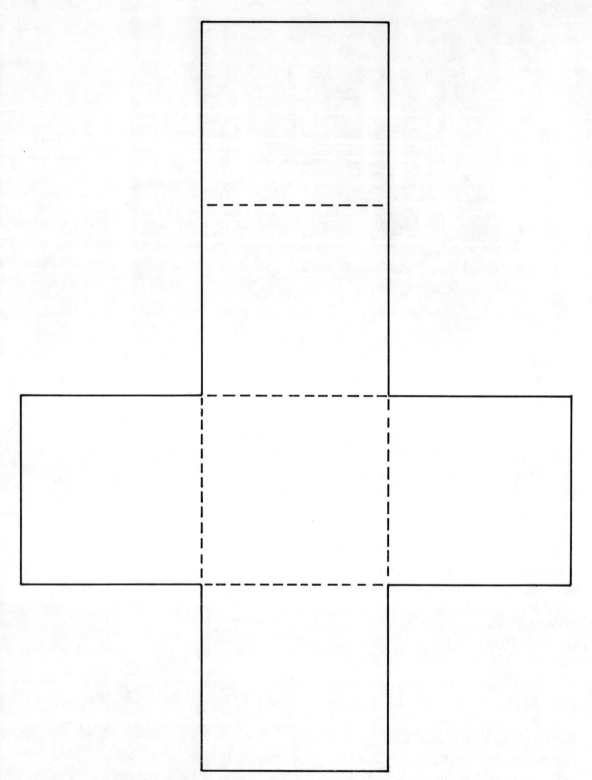

FOLD ON DOTTED LINES

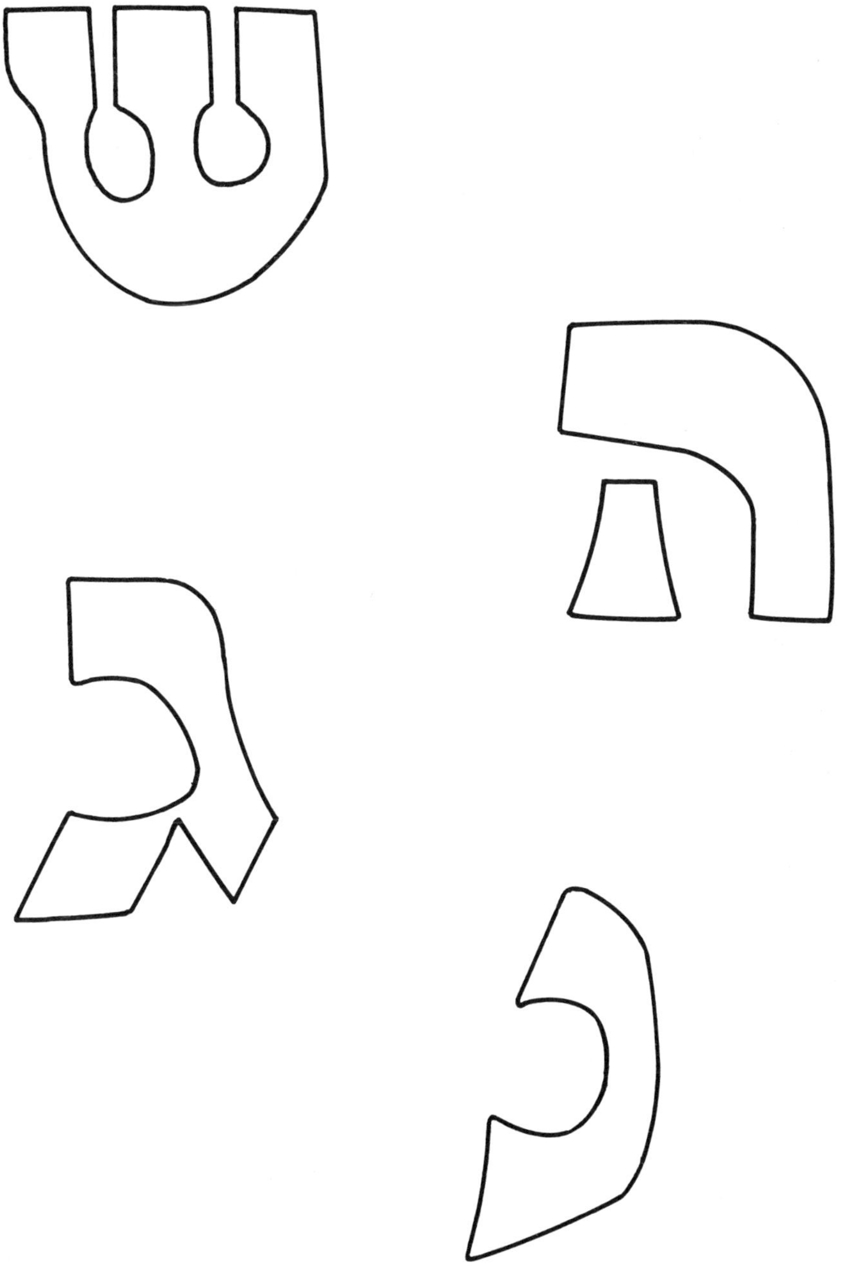
ש
ה
ג
נ

HANUKKAH GREETING CARDS

ALTHOUGH you wouldn't want to make dozens of greeting cards for the holiday season, making a few special ones for close friends and relatives can be very satisfying.

If you start with a plain card of good quality, with matching envelope, your own creation will have a professional look. These plain cards, in shades of blue, beige, gray, and white, are available at art-supply stores, and although they are not especially cheap, they are not as expensive as really fine greeting cards commercially made.

Here are a few suggested designs. Since the menorah is one of the most important symbols of the season, I've made designs of nine candles in various shapes. If you use a stencil and a colored felt pen, you will end up with a professional-looking handcrafted card.

You can buy stencils of various shapes in packages at art-supply shops. You can also make up your own designs and cut your own stencils in a heavy waxed stencil paper, also available at art-supply shops. For my cards I used the shapes in the sides and bottoms of the small plastic baskets from the market, the kind of baskets that cherry tomatoes come in. When the basket is cut apart, it can be used as a stencil by combining one section with another. To make the nine candles of the menorah, I had to move the stencil two or three times.

These plastic baskets come with different designs. Ask your grocer for one of each, and you will have enough stencil designs to create many different greeting cards.

For colors, I chose to make my complete design in dark blue on gray for one card; another of green "candles" with red "flames" for a card of gray; and the third, a blue card, with candles of purple and flames of rose.

GIFT-WRAPPING PAPER
.FOR HANUKKAH

GIFT-WRAPPING paper for Hanukkah is not easy to find. But it is easy to make, with a little time and ingenuity, and a bit of colored ink.

Cut a piece of regular brown wrapping paper to fit your gift package, and decorate it with stencils or with designs cut into Styrofoam pieces.

To make your Styrofoam stamps, choose your design and trace it onto a piece of the plastic tray that meat comes on. Cut out the stamp, and make heavy lines with a pencil where you want them to show. Use stamp pads such as those used in offices and post offices. These are available in red, green, blue, purple, and black. Stamp your design onto your wrapping paper, and tie it with ribbon of a color to match the design.

If you prefer to use stencils, color your designs with felt pens. Cut your stencils from regular waxed stencil paper, or use the sides and bottoms of the plastic baskets that fruit and cherry tomatoes come in.

You will not want to make great quantities of such decorated wrapping paper, but try some for a few of your very special gifts.

Christmas Day

December 25

CHRISTMAS DAY is celebrated throughout the Christian world as the birthday of Jesus, though the exact date of His birth has never been accurately determined. Perhaps a date in late December was chosen because it is the time of year when the days begin to lengthen and the light grows stronger after the dark days of November, and symbolically, the life of Jesus gives light to the world.

The holiday is celebrated in the churches with a midnight candlelight service on Christmas Eve and services on Christmas Day. Carols are important in these services. One of the best loved is "Silent Night," a carol written in 1818 by Joseph Mohr of Oberndorf, Austria. The same night that it was written it was sung at the midnight mass.

Many of our Christmas customs come to us from Europe. The Santa Claus who brings presents to the children is patterned after St. Nicholas. The Christmas tree, perhaps the most popular of all Christmas symbols, comes from Germany. Dutch children leave a wooden shoe by the fireplace for St. Nicholas to fill with gifts. The Yule logs, the plum pudding, and many of the carols came to us from England, as did the custom of exchanging Christmas cards, a Victorian tradition that originated in London in 1843.

Christmas is a festive time of parties, gift giving, and the exchange of good wishes between friends, and the holiday decorations in cities and towns are as colorful as those in our homes.

A CHRISTMAS CENTERPIECE

TRADITIONALLY, an apple pyramid at Christmas time is a symbol of hospitality. It was used during the eighteenth and nineteenth centuries, and comes to us from England.

Here's a fruit pyramid that has lemons and limes as well as apples for a variation of color, and with sprigs of holly to fill the spaces in between the fruit.

You will need about 15 apples and 8 or 10 lemons and the same number of limes. You will also need about 5′ of 4-gauge iron wire.

Start with a Styrofoam cone 12″ high. Polish your apples before you attach them to the cone. The bottom row will take about 7 apples.

Cut a piece of wire about 4″ long, spear the apple onto one end, and insert the other end into the cone. Put the wire into the blossom end of the apple so the stem end shows. The second row will take 6 apples, and the third, 5. When you get up to the fourth row, alternate apples with lemons and limes for added color. As the cone becomes narrower, cut your wire pieces shorter so they won't come through the cone.

If your grocer has lady apples, as some shops do at Christmas time, use those for the smaller part of the cone, and mix them with the lemons and limes.

For the very top of the cone, attach a lady apple or a lemon—unless you happen to be able to find a small pineapple. That is the ultimate in hospitality, but a small one is required to fit the style and size of the other fruits. If you have a pineapple, use only the top third.

After you have built up your pyramid, break off small sprigs of holly from large branches (or use other evergreens from your garden), and insert them into the spaces between the fruits. Place your pyramid on a tray that is larger than the bottom of the centerpiece, and place a border of greens around the tray. The pyramid will last for more than a week.

CHRISTMAS ADVENT CALENDAR

AN Advent Calendar to mark the days from the first of December to Christmas Eve is easy to make if you have a supply of old Christmas cards at hand. The golds and silvers, the designs and trimmings on cards finish the shutters of the calendar's windows and trim the edges of the house.

Start with a sheet of dark blue construction paper 9″ by 12″. Draw a line through the center, lengthwise, on the wrong side of the paper to serve as a guide.

Measure down on each side 4″ and draw a line from that point to the center of the top. This will form the roof. Draw in the chimney about midway down one side of the peak—the chimney is 1¼″ wide—and cut out the house. It will be

9″ wide and 12″ tall at the center of the roof's peak.

On the right side of the paper, mark off the windows, starting 3″ down from the top of the roof. All windows are ¾″ wide and ¾″ tall, except the 3 in the third row. These are 1″ tall and ¾″ wide, just for variation.

Leave ½″ between all windows, and about ¼″ between the rows, and center your rows on the house, leaving the same amount of space on each side.

The door is 1½″ wide and 1½″ tall.

With an X-Acto knife and a ruler edge, cut across the top and bottom of all windows and the door, and then down through the center of each. Bend back the shutters. *Don't* cut down each

side of your windows, or you will loose your shutters.

Paste on strips of gold or colored designs from old Christmas cards, trimming each row of shutters with the same color. Use stick glue—it will not mar the paper.

Trim the edges of the roof and the walls of the house with strips of gold, and top the chimney with gold.

Cover the door with gold pieces; give the door and the windows on each side of it a triangular lintel of gold, and paste 2 golden steps below the door.

On the back of the calendar paste a lining of red shelf paper, placing it so the red side of the paper will show through the little windows. Use stick

glue and fasten the red paper securely.

In each little window paste a tiny picture cut from a Christmas card—a toy, an animal, a candle, or whatever you can find. Paste the cutout onto the red shelf paper. In the doorway paste a Christmas tree.

Starting on December 1, one window should be opened each day, until on the twentieth-fourth the door is opened, and there is the Christmas tree.

When all the windows are open, stand the calendar in front of a lamp. The light will shine through the red paper, giving the little house a Christmas glow.

MEDIEVAL CHRISTMAS CASTLE

THIS is what an English friend of mine calls a "proper castle." It has turrets and towers and ramparts, and a courtyard where knights in armor ride on their panoplied horses.

Place the castle under the Christmas tree or on a mantel. Or use it for other times of the year, too, when you want a "story" centerpiece.

For the towers, save soup cans, coffee cans, and all kinds of cans of various sizes. Cover them with construction paper (use stick glue), and in constrast-

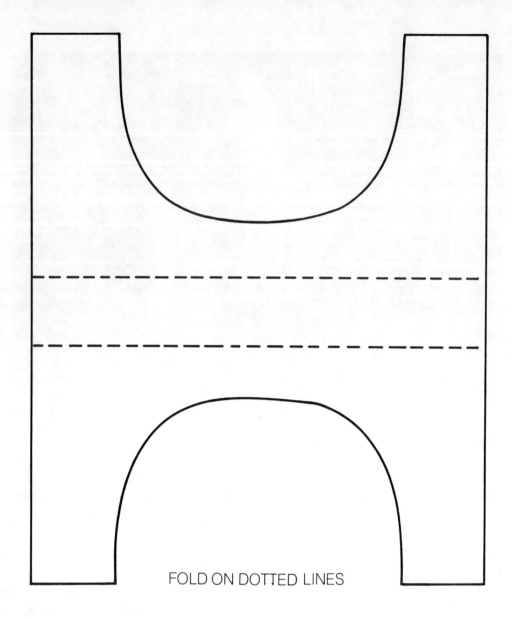

FOLD ON DOTTED LINES

ing colors paste on small pieces for windows and doors. Top the towers with cone-shaped roofs made of about a third of a circle of construction paper. Experiment in newspaper until you find the right size to fit your tower.

For the tallest tower I taped 2 soup cans together with masking tape, and then covered them with paper.

Small boxes, also covered with paper, make up part of the castle wall. For each end of the box paste on peaked pieces to form the gables that hold up the roof. Cut them to fit the side of the box and extend the paper 1″ or so for the peak.

The roof is an oblong piece of paper folded in half and fitted over the end gables, secured with stick glue. Paste on snips of paper for doors and windows.

The cardboard bridges are covered with construction paper. Follow the pattern given here. Cover the sides of the walls with construction paper that extends up beyond the bridge itself, and snip it to simulate a crenelated wall.

The ramparts are made in the same way, but without the opening that forms the bridge.

Arrange the various towers, houses, and ramparts on a large base—I used a large piece of dark construction paper—

in a sort of circle, to make the court-yard.

You can add as many towers and ramparts as you like, and you can add to it year by year. The various sections are easily packed away, to be used again and again.

CHRISTMAS CRÈCHE

HERE is a Christmas crèche that will fit on a mantel or under a Christmas tree, and you probably have all the ingredients right at hand.

The little shelter is made of card-

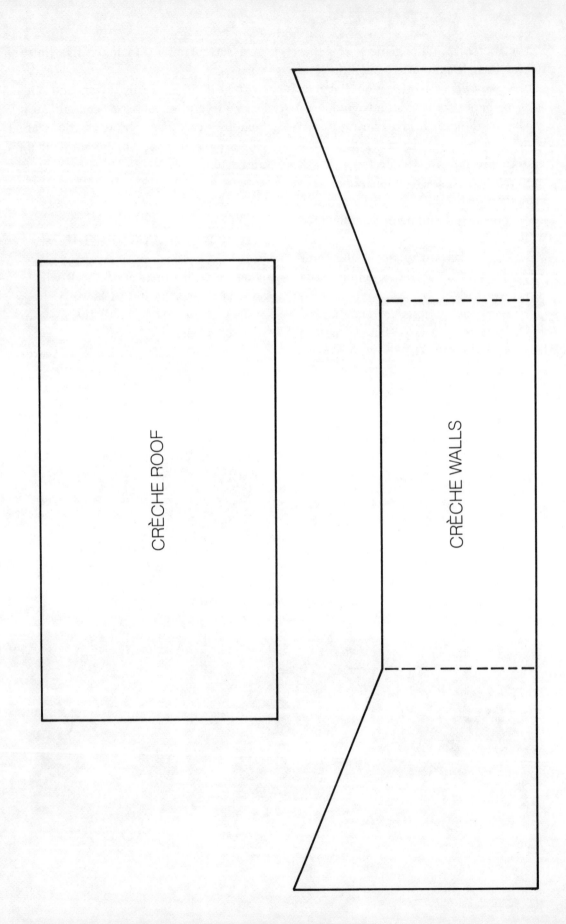

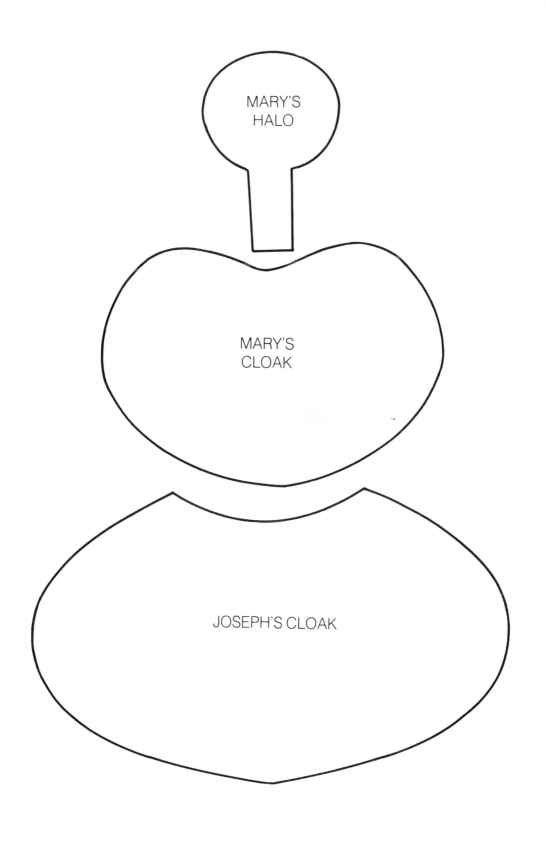

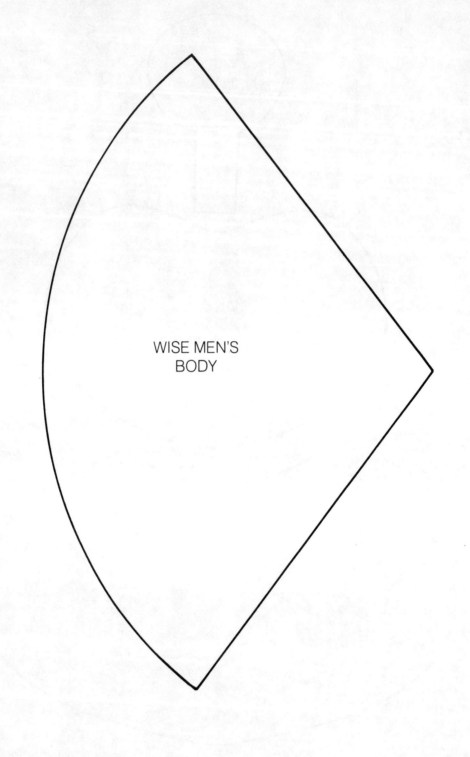

WISE MEN'S
BODY

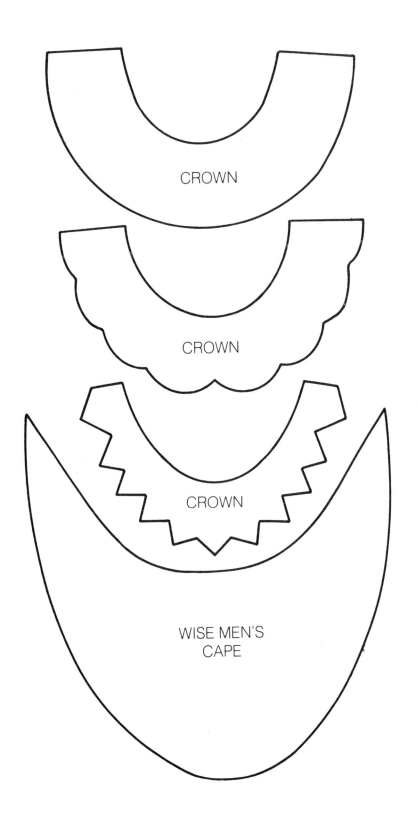

CROWN

CROWN

CROWN

WISE MEN'S
CAPE

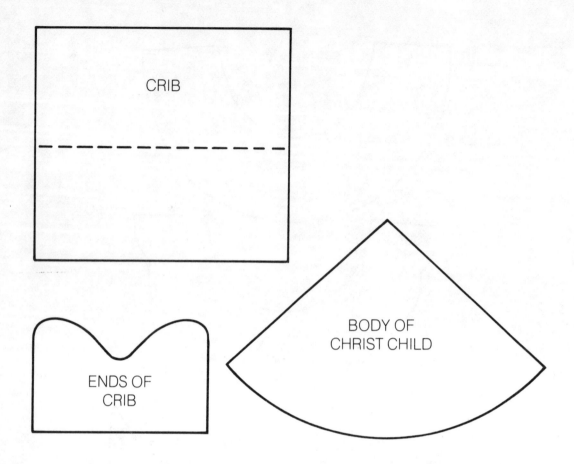

CRIB

ENDS OF
CRIB

BODY OF
CHRIST CHILD

board wound with rough-textured cord. For the shape of the shelter, follow the dimensions given in the drawing. As you wind the cord, secure it with white glue. Finish off the edges of the walls with braided cord.

The roof is a separate piece that simply rests on top of the three-sided stable. The stable itself is made of one piece of cardboard, folded to form three sides. The floor is simply a piece of dark construction paper a little larger than the stable.

All the figures are made of construction paper cones, with hazelnuts for heads. Joseph's costume is brown with a yellow cape. He has a black-yarn beard and hair, put on with glue, and black eyes drawn with a felt pen.

Make the body of a half-circle 9″ in diameter. Form into a cone and snip off the top ½″ so the head will fit securely. Attach the hazelnut head to the body with white glue.

For his cape, follow the pattern given and glue it to the body.

Mary's body is light blue construction paper. Use a half-circle about 7″ in diameter, form a cone, secure with stick glue, and snip off the top ½″. Glue a hazelnut to the cone for a head—find a smaller one than Joseph's if you can—and for this use white glue. With a dark blue ball-point pen, draw her features. Fasten yellow yarn to the head for hair.

Mary's cloak (follow the pattern given) is attached to the body with stick glue. From yellow construction paper—or gold paper if it is gold on both sides—cut a halo for Mary, following the pattern here. Glue to the back of the body.

The three wise men are made of construction paper—one purple, one blue, and one pink, with contrasting cloaks and golden crowns. Start with a third of a circle 8″ in diameter, form into a cone, fasten with stick glue.

Each crown is different. The patterns are given here. Trim the crowns with self-adhesive gold braid, and put gold braid around the three men's necks.

The hair of the wise men is drawn on with a black felt pen. After the hair is dry, glue their crowns on with one of the white glue.

The crib for the Christ Child is made from three pieces of cardboard trimmed with the same rough-textured cord that covers the stable (see drawing for pattern).

The Christ Child is made of yellow construction paper. Use a quarter of a circle that is 4½″ in diameter, shape into a cone and fasten with stick glue. Snip off ¼″ at the top of the cone, glue on a small nut—I used an acorn—for the head, draw closed eyes, and attach a ring of gold braid for a halo. Fill the crib with cotton batting, and place the figure on it.

The little wooden animals are some I have collected on my travels. These came from the little town of Bethlehem and so seemed especially appropriate for the crèche.

CHRISTMAS CARDS

MAKING Christmas cards for a few favored friends can give an added mean-

ing to the holiday season. Here are a few suggestions.

Start with a plain card and matching envelope. These are available in various colors in art-supply shops. They give a finished look to your own creations. If you can't find such cards, use a good quality of construction paper, and cut a card, folded double, to fit a standard-sized envelope.

Make your designs with lace paper doilies—perhaps the gold or silver ones—and paste them onto the card with stick glue, which will not mar the card or the cutout. For a Christmas tree design, use the edges of the doily, and paste a "star" at the top of the tree.

The scene of ancient Bethlehem is cut from colored metallic paper, with a large star of gold. The snowflake de-signs are cut from plastic by-the-yard place mats available in five-and-ten-cent stores. A triangle of lace forms a tree, with small white plastic sequins pasted on for stars. And the tree of lace has four tiers, each one cut a little larger than the one above.

For the three Kings, cut triangles of bright-colored shiny paper, and trim them with crowns and edgings of lace paper doilies. And if you find stencils of wintery scenes in your local stationery store or art-supply shop, use these to make colorful cards with the help of colored felt pens.

Once you have started cutting and planning your designs, you will find it hard to stop, and you will end up with many more cards and designs than you had anticipated.

For All Occasions

ANY occasions that are not specific holidays are often given
greater significance with the addition of a bouquet, a set
of place cards, unusual favors, a particular greeting. Here are a
few suggestions for those birthdays, family gatherings, gradua-
tions, and other kinds of celebrations that are not actual holidays
but are as important to us when they occur.

FANCY FLOWERS

MANY kinds of material can be made
into flowers—from paper to calico, and
from ribbons to lace.

For the calico flowers, cut strips on
the bias, 4" wide and 12" long. Fold the
strip in half lengthwise, and proceed as
with the Mother's Day rosebuds. Use
12-gauge iron wire or long pipe cleaners
for stems. Mix the colors and patterns of
fabric for a varied bouquet.

Calico flowers make an early American bouquet—for the Fourth of July
table, the Halloween table, or the American Indian Day table.

Lace flowers have an elegant air
about them and are suitable for a table
set for tea.

Laces come in different widths and
designs and in a variety of shades. Some
laces are gathered, some straight. The
gathered ones make full-blown flowers,
the straight are fine for making buds.
Make them just as the rosebuds are
made, and wind your finished flowers
onto pipe-cleaner stems with floral tape.
Give each flower two or three leaves.

For a peonylike flower I used a 3"
wide white lace that has a red pattern
running through it and red scalloped
edges. It took about 30" of lace to make
a flower 4" across.

Tissue paper, too, can be used for
flowers. A chrysanthemumlike blossom
is made with long strips, fringed and
wound onto a wire stem. These should
be very full and about 2" across.

171

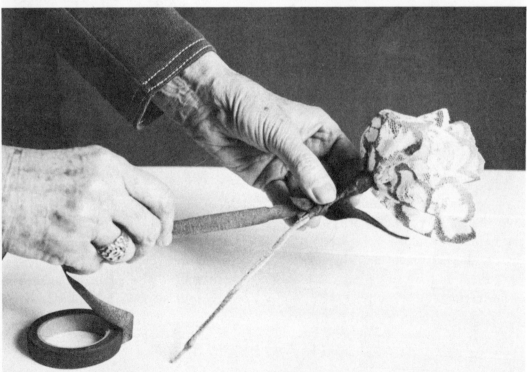

ALL-SEASON STATIONERY

NOTE paper for all occasions can be made with the help of last year's greeting cards—Christmas cards, valentines, birthday cards, and other treasures saved from the wastebasket. Stenciling, too, gives color and distinction to plain writing paper.

Starting with plain note paper and envelopes, you can follow a theme or make colorful designs. Stick glue works well for pasting on cutouts; a felt pen will easily put on a stenciled design.

Here are a few suggestions: a set of correspondence cards with animal cutouts, perhaps for a child who likes animals; note paper with cutouts of children; cards with Christmas symbols. And for birdwatchers, you might use cutouts of the many kinds of birds found on all sorts of greeting cards.

If you use stencils, the envelope can easily be decorated too.

DECORATIVE PLACE CARDS

PLACE cards trim a party table and are easy to put together. Here is a series of them ready for a Christmas dinner table. These designs came from last year's cards. By choosing your cutouts with a certain occasion in mind, you can suit your place cards to the event—for all sorts of holidays, birthdays, family dinner parties, luncheons, and tea par-

ties. Make them ahead of time and store them flat.

Start with a 4″ square card or heavy white paper—or colored paper, if you prefer—and fold it in half so it will stand up. Paste cutouts on the cards—cutouts no more than 4″ tall but tall enough to extend beyond the fold. Attach with stick glue, placing the design to one side so there will be space for the guest's name.

These can be made in sets to be given as gifts for occasions all around the year.

YARN PEOPLE FOR PARTY FAVORS

I CALL these little yarn figures the ten-minute favors because they are so quick and easy to make. Use them for party favors, for mobiles, to tie to gift packages, or to hang on the Christmas tree.

Start with yarn of whatever color you like—I prefer white—and wind it about 50 times around a 6″ piece of cardboard, or around your outstretched fingers. Tie a contrasting piece of yarn about the "neck."

Then wind yarn around a 3½″ piece of cardboard—or around your loosely opened-up fingers—for the arms. Tie both ends at the wrist. Divide the body yarn in half, front and back, and slip the arms through. Then tie the waist, just below the arms. Thus the arms are held securely between the neck and the waist.

If your figure is to be a boy, divide the body yarn into two legs, and tie at the ankles. If it is to be a girl, trim off the bottom to form a skirt.

Give your little girl a babushka and a skirt of calico or colored felt. And make a cone-shaped hat for the boy, using bright felt or calico. And if you plan to hang the figures on a mobile or on the Christmas tree, attach a piece of black thread to the top of the peaked hat and to the girls' scarves.

177

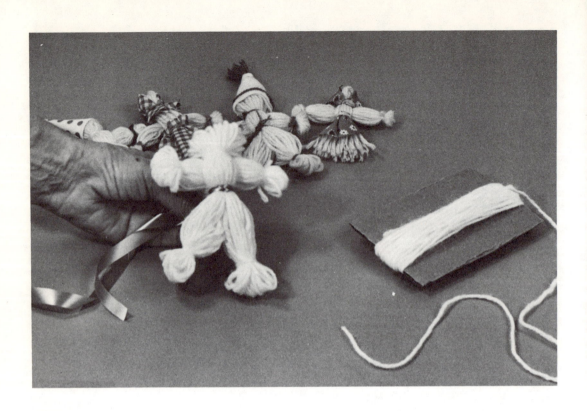

A HANDY PAIR OF GIFTS
FOR THE KITCHEN

HERE is a nice combination to make for a house-warming gift, a shower gift, or a hostess gift. Both the tray holder and the potholder come from Scandinavia, and both are interesting, colorful, and useful.

Hang your trays on the wall with a decorative tray holder. You will need 2¼ yards of heavy tape that is 3″ wide. Sew the ends of the tape together, double it, and slip through a 3″ ring of wood, plastic, or brass. (Curtain rings are useful for this.) This will give you two loops, one on each side of the ring, about 20″ long.

Put a few stitches through the 4 layers of fabric just under the ring, slightly spreading the loops apart, and hang the tray holder on a wall hook. The tapes will hold two, three, or more trays —and at the same time add color to the kitchen.

To decorate the tray holder, cut out shapes of peaches (as on mine) or strawberries (as on the tray holder made of upholstery webbing), and use self-adhesive felt for the designs. If you can't fine the self-adhesive kind, cut your shapes from regular felt and glue them onto the tray tapes.

A companion piece from Scandinavia is the potholder that slips over the han-

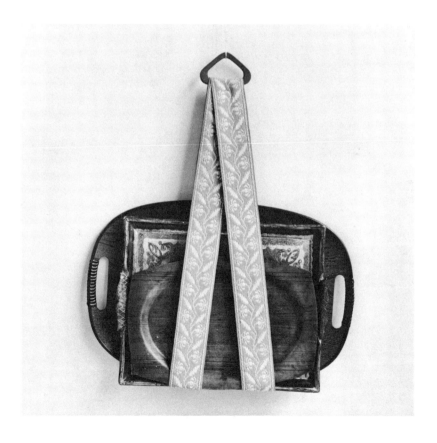

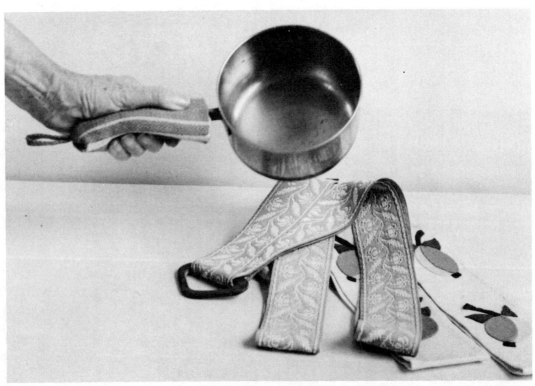

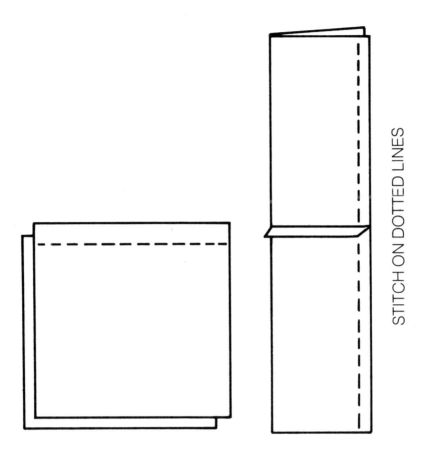

STITCH ON DOTTED LINES

dle of a pot. Cut a piece of colorful, sturdy fabric about 6″ square. Cut a double piece of white felt for the lining. Sew the lining to the *wrong* side of the fabric, running the seam along one side of the square. Open it up, fold lengthwise and stitch to form tube. (See diagram.) Turn right side out, fold the open end together, slip in a loop of tape to hang it up by, and stitch along the folded closed end.

If you use colors to go with your tray holder, the two will make a useful and welcome pair.

181

FANCY GIFT BOXES

THE box is sometimes the most important part of a gift. Save your sturdy boxes, and decorate them for those occasions when something special is needed.

I covered one of my boxes with wide pink satin ribbon, and then glued strips of pink flowered lace over the ribbon. On the top I pasted a pink, flat, velvet bow.

Another was covered with white satin material and then trimmed with blue flowered lace. Either of these would be suitable for a Mother's Day or birthday gift.

For less-elegant boxes, use colored paper or gift-wrapping paper. Shelf paper of various colors, too, makes fine coverings for boxes, and these can be decorated with cutouts from cards—Christmas motifs, or any number of other designs for other occasions.

SOURCES FOR MATERIALS

ONE of the best sources for craft materials is the great variety of packaging found today. Cans, boxes, plastic containers, and paper of many kinds and colors come home with us from the market, and all too often they are tossed away without a further thought. Many of these materials can be put to second uses with a little patience and imagination.

Construction paper comes in packages of fifty sheets of assorted colors in two sizes—9″ by 12″, and 12″ by 18″. The larger size is more useful and is found in art-supply shops.

Metallic paper, which is a light-weight cardboard coated with metallic colors on one side, comes in sheets 36″ square and is sold in art-supply shops.

Crepe paper and tissue paper, in solid colors and in shaded tones, is available in all dime and stationery shops; look for regular white typing paper at your corner stationery shop.

There are many kinds of glue on the market today. I have found the stick glues to be especially good with paper—particularly if the paper is fragile. The white glues are useful, and the new Titebond—a variation of white glue—dries more quickly and holds better than the more familiar kinds. All of these are available at stationery, hardware, and art-supply shops, and in some dime stores.

Squares of felt in many colors come in packages of two dozen in dime stores and hobby shops. Felt also comes by the yard in department stores.

Squares of self-adhesive felt and burlap in various colors are sold in hobby shops. Gold and silver cord wound on cards in cellophane packages is sold in department stores and sewing supply shops. Large spools of cord can be found in greeting card shops.

Look in your local hobby store for sheets of copper. It comes in strips 12″ wide and a yard or more long, and in varying weights. I like the 36-gauge weight.

Your hardware shop will have wire in small quantities—both copper wire and regular iron wire. Both come in 6″ lengths wound on cards in varying gauges from very fine to extra heavy.

Floral tape and floral clay are sold in hobby shops, florists' shops, and some dime stores.

Store your decorations for another year in sturdy cartons, and attach a label listing the contents. Use masking tape to secure the cover and keep out the dust.

Index